MOTHERING
as a
SPIRITUAL JOURNEY

Also by Ann Tremaine Linthorst...

A Gift of Love: Marriage as a Spiritual Journey

Thus Saith the Lord, Giddyap!
Commentaries on Human Experience and Spiritual Growth

MOTHERING
as a
SPIRITUAL JOURNEY

——— ?&. ———

Learning to Let God
Nurture Your Children
and You Along with Them

ANN TREMAINE LINTHORST

CROSSROAD · NEW YORK

This printing: 1998

The Crossroad Publishing Company
370 Lexington Avenue, New York, NY 10017

Copyright © 1993 by Ann Tremaine Linthorst

Printed in the United States of America

Library of Congress Cataloging-in-Publication Data

Mothering as a spiritual journey : learning to let God nurture
your children and you along with them / Ann Tremaine Linthorst.
    p. cm.
  ISBN 0-8245-1250-2 (pbk.)
    1. Mothers—Religious life. 2. Mother and child. I. Title.
BV4529.L56 1993
248.8′431—dc20   92-16593
                                         CIP

For my mother, Mary...
For my sons, Thomas Anton and Erik Jan...
And for Jan: husband, father, lover, teacher, friend...

ADORABLE ONE(S)

And He shall give His angels charge over thee, to keep thee in all thy ways.

—Psalm 91

Contents

Chapter 6
YOUNG ADULTHOOD: The Crisis of Loss / The Marvel of Divine Completeness

Acknowledgments

The unfoldment of this book has been facilitated by many people whose input, encouragement, support, and guidance have been an important part of its blooming. I want to thank Jan Kovac and Jill Gustavson, friends and mothers, for their time and guidance; Joan Taylor, for her substantial, professional editing and for respecting me enough to criticize me like a peer; Natasha Kern for goading me; and Susan Schwartz for nurturing me toward the necessary rewrite.

I am grateful to have found, at Crossroad, Michael Leach, who readily agreed to publish the book, not because it guaranteed him big bucks but because he believed in it. Thanks to Kyle Elaine Miller for shepherding me along with the details, and the rest of the gang there, for doing their jobs well and being committed to publishing quality ideas.

Great appreciation goes to Polly Berends and Marianne Williamson, spiritual authors of great stature themselves, for reading and gracing the book with their blessings; and to Rev. Peggy Bassett for her enthusiastic reading and support.

And to all those who supported the work, even before it was judged commercially acceptable, especially Maureen Cronin and Roland Seboldt: your encouragement meant more than I can say.

Introduction

The experiences of human motherhood share in a universal dimension, however personal and distinct they seem to each mother. Each stage of child development is equally a stage in a mother's development. Humanly, each stage has its particular stresses and horrors, as well as its peculiar joys and rewards. Motherhood is much harder than a non-mother could ever believe, and nothing we read about it before we experience it can quite prepare us for the subjective suffering to which certain stages inevitably give rise.

But behind and within the human experience of motherhood lies the spiritual Reality of things, God. Although we start out thinking that we are in this life to get what we want and to make our dreams come true, if we are lucky we discover that these things are the least of it. Life is not here for us, but we are here for Life, in the largest, capital "L" meaning of the word. To quote Rabbi Nachmann of Bratzlav: "As the hand held before the eye conceals the greatest mountain, so the little earthly life hides from the glance the enormous lights and mysteries of which the world is full, and he who can draw it away from before his eyes, as one draws away a hand, beholds the great shining of the inner worlds."

This might sound as if we must give up normal human activities such as marriage and parenthood to discover "the great shining of the inner worlds." But that is not the case. Rather, being interested in the "lights and mysteries" of Life, we can discover them within the heart of our most cherished human experiences. And as we make such discoveries, we find the stuff of our daily lives enhanced and facilitated and fulfilled. When we become aware, in the slightest degree, that our little human experience is not the last word on the situation, we find the door opened to a power for good that meets the details of our needs in the most practical ways. The fact that we live and move and have our Being in a spiritual realm of pure Love, pure Intelligence, pure Goodness, is the basis upon which we find every detail of the human scene sanctified, supported, and protected.

Mothering as a personal, human story is often experienced as a series of crises. But when we regard mothering as a spiritual journey, we find that each crisis may yield for us a blessing of spiritual growth and discovery. Motherhood's crises are marvelous, and motherhood, as a context for spiritual discovery, is unsurpassed by any other form of spiritual life or commitment. One of my teachers once commented that he knew of only one group of people who were motivated to become enlightened for the sake of others — and that was mothers, for their children.

My own journey has taken me through traditional Christian belief and traditional psychology to the spiritually oriented psychiatry of Thomas Hora, in which I first found these fields unified in the oneness of spiritual consciousness. During my two decades of research in Dr. Hora's system of thought, I was also greatly nurtured by the study of the writings of Joel Goldsmith, Eric Butterworth, Krishnamurti, Zen Buddhism, and Christian Science. Throughout these studies, the ongoing discovery has been of God, spiritual Good, as the truth of Life, hence the truth of my life, here and now. Getting clear that Life is God-governed and God-constituted has enabled me, more and more, to let God nurture and raise my children and has led me to feel increasingly supported and nurtured by the divine Presence as well.

The ideas presented in this book are those that have sustained, guided, inspired, and rescued me through twenty years of motherhood. A friend who read the manuscript commented, "Of course, you have not had any of the terrible problems that many parents have." Exactly! That is what motivates the sharing of these truthful ideas with others. We do not need to be passive victims of any and every horror that the human sense of motherhood can dredge up. No matter what mental equipment we bring, humanly, to motherhood, a spiritual orientation toward Life brings the light of truth to all aspects of motherhood. It is because of this spiritual context that I can look back on my two decades of active mothering with gratitude.

> I am grateful to have had the opportunity to let motherhood qualities be expressed through me. I feel so much enriched and secured by the seeing and being that have taken place because of being a mother. Despite my personal fears and tightness and grouchiness, Love has looked lovingly through my eyes at my children; intelligence has responded helpfully to their needs; vitality has joined them in their adventures and their play.
>
> To the eye of one unfamiliar with children, they often appear as an unknown species. I have loved seeing the masks of unfamiliarity dissolve, so that babies and toddlers and little kids and big kids and teenagers and young adults now all seem like friends to me, not strangers. My own children have made me one with all children.
>
> I am grateful to have had the opportunity to let childness qualities fill my adult years. I am more flexible, open, spontaneous, and playful because of having had children. And, though it may seem contradictory, I am also more mature, centered, decisive, and sure of myself. There is no conflict, spiritually, between childness and maturity; they are two aspects of the completeness of Being.

I am grateful to have had the expansion of consciousness invited and evoked and cajoled in the
positive and delightful ways that only motherhood
provides.

This statement of gratitude also ends the book. It is presented here as an introduction to the possibilities that this
particular spiritual journey unfolds for us. The reader is offered that journey, in brief, through the reading of the book,
so that this statement is rediscovered at the end, filled with
the meaning learned in the process. In just this way is the
promise of motherhood fulfilled through crises yielding to
marvels, step by step, in the growing awareness of Life as
divine.

Chapter 1

The Marvelous Journey of Motherhood

A friend and I were talking together. We each have two sons and have both been very involved mothers. I had just sent my second son off to college, and her older boy had been gone a month. She had been in tears a lot since he left and was asking me what it was like to have both children gone. I was trying to be encouraging, for my own sake as well as hers.

"Well, in some ways it's really nice . . . " I began.

I was going to comment on the spaciousness, peace, and order in the house, without the presence of two teenage males, but she interrupted me.

"No, it's not!" she exclaimed, whacking me on the arm. "Your kids are gone!"

And she burst into tears.

Being a mother is a funny thing: you cry when the children arrive, you cry when they leave, and you cry a lot in between. But you wouldn't trade the experience for anything in the world. Last fall I sent my second son off to college, a year after the first boy left. It was all according to plan, good for everybody. Yet it felt like a crisis to me for some months. And as I thought back to the beginnings of motherhood, I remembered what a crisis it was when two babies arrived, sixteen months apart. From first to last, motherhood is one crisis after another.

And, from first to last, motherhood is one marvel after another as well. In fact, the crises and the marvels go hand in hand. A "crisis" is defined as a "turning point," and a marvel is "a wonderful or astonishing thing or miracle." I like to think of a marvel as an event that tells us something wonderful about Life. Life is spelled with a capital "L" to show that it points to something beyond what we can see from our ordinary human standpoint. A marvel expands our awareness of what Life is. It shows us the divine realities that are always here, though partially hidden by the personal interpretation of things. *The marvelous crises of motherhood are opportunities to notice, through the experiences of motherhood, that Life is bigger and better than we have been able to notice before.*

I was already both a professional counselor and a spiritual student before I became a mother. So I have been blessed with the necessity to observe motherhood for the purpose of helping others with it. This has provided me with a certain distance from my own experiences and an extra incentive to find the positive possibilities that heal and resolve the seeming problems along the way. I have found my spiritual studies of such consistent help and assurance that I wonder how any woman survives without some context of faith or spiritual understanding. I have also noticed that the nature of the mother/child experience so profoundly illustrates the larger spiritual realities of Life that many women grow spiritually through the process without ever consciously realizing what is happening. Yet it is even better to be able to notice, step by step, the tangible evidences of a larger Good.

Motherhood Is a Journey of Transcendental Discovery

The spiritual journey of motherhood looks beyond the interpersonal story of a mother and a baby to see the universal truths underlying and manifesting through the human experiences. Being a mother is thus lifted off the nuts-and-bolts level of the management of children to a level of transcendental discovery that incidentally blesses and enhances the human experience at every point. None of us starts out knowing how to be a mother. The experience makes the mother by allowing her to discover her qualities and capacities from that particular standpoint. Likewise, no one starts out understanding what it means that "God is Love." But if we go into motherhood seeing it as a process of spiritual growth and discovery, we will find each stage teaching us more about Love as a reality that is present even when we personally can't seem to come up with it. We will discover that it is this divine Love and Intelligence that raises our children. And, in that discovery, we will find ourselves divinely nurtured and matured as well.

Having "Eyes to See" Turns Crises into Marvels

The marvelous expansion of awareness called being a mother feels like a crisis to our human sense of ourselves at every point where that old sense is challenged by the new unfoldment. It is the nature of human ego sense to resist change because it alters our picture of who and what we are. And we like to be certain of who we are, even if the picture isn't altogether positive. By definition then, ego sense strives to keep its view of things constant, and this means limited. It feels comfortable only with the known, and what doesn't fit its picture will make it feel uncomfortable. Yet expansion is the nature of Life, because Life lives to bloom. Seeing more and more of what really is — despite the human, limited beliefs — is what makes our human experiences fruitful and fulfilled. We bloom by seeing.

Unfortunately, such discoveries do not automatically happen along with physical growth. We must "have eyes" to see the spiritual realm. "Having eyes" is a matter of learning to look at things from a different angle — from the divine angle. To the human sense of motherhood, suffering is inherent. Pain and motherhood are thought to be virtually synonymous. From the "travail" of childbirth to the anguish of the child's departure, the lot of mothers is considered to be a hard one. But the whole of the human experience is fraught with suffering until we learn to look at Life from a standpoint different from that of the little personal ego.

Suffering is a product of the personal misconception of things. That misconception says life comes in little material fragments, containing a few qualities but lacking others. We all want quality life more than anything else. But we are misled by the human misconception of things into believing that the qualities must come through other people or situations. Persons are everlastingly trying to get more good qualities from other little bits of life. The human myth around motherhood is just such a belief: "I will be happy and fulfilled if I have a baby." We quickly discover that just getting babies does not, per se, make us happy. It does not, per se, give us quality life.

Discovering Quality Identity

When we think a baby will make us happy, what kind of life are we picturing? My own sense of what being a mother would give me had to do with my experiences as a babysitter in college. I liked the kinds of qualities that came up in me around small children. I found myself more loving and playful and creative when I was babysitting than I seemed to be in other areas of my life as a young adult. And when my favorite toddler-charge came running to me with his arms outstretched, I felt confirmed as someone of worth and goodness.

I think, then, that we want to be mothers because children seem to give us the chance to experience ourselves as loving and good in ways not otherwise available. The big shock and disappointment of children is that we sometimes find children provoke our worst selves, rather than our best selves. This is not unlike the shock of discovering that the man we married can make us feel terrible as well as wonderful. Both experiences point to the fact that our sense of positive identity must be based on something more reliable than other people's behavior.

How do we know who we truly are, and how do we help our children know who they truly are? Interpersonal psychology places great emphasis on the role of others in establishing self-esteem. There are books written to tell mothers how to raise children so that they have self-esteem, yet we know intuitively that we must have it ourselves before we can pass it on to our kids. And if we go by other people's behavior toward us and ours toward them, we will always have cause to doubt ourselves.

We know who we truly are when we know what divine Life is, and we begin to discover the nature of divine Life when we think in terms of qualities. Asking ourselves what qualities are good, we spontaneously come up with such things as love, beauty, harmony, peace, intelligence, grace, purity, and innocence. The fact that we can name such qualities, whether or not we think they have been part of our personal experience, gives evidence of the universal nature of such qualities. They exist as attributes of spiritual Life. They belong to us because we are made "in the image and likeness" of God. "It is He that hath made us and not we ourselves" (Ps. 100). We look to God for our quality identity rather than to other persons.

The personal self may not be estimable, but the qualities that make up our true identity are always worthy of the highest esteem. This is so because they are divine qualities, not personal ones. *Therefore, we do not need to have self-esteem;*

we need to discover quality identity. When we think of identity in quality terms, then we find it to be something that is discovered rather than something that others can bestow upon us or withhold from us. We see spiritual qualities when we look for them. "Beauty is in the eye of the beholder," says the old adage. And not only beauty, but love and grace and all the rest. We must consciously learn to think and see in terms of qualities rather than personalities before we will feel the security and assurance of an unchanging basis of identity, for ourselves and our children.

The Value of the God-Context

The God-context provides us with greater resources for mothering than our human background and personal beliefs could allow. We want to know how to be better, happier, freer mothers than our own mothers were able to be, even if they were good mothers. We can be. This does not dishonor our mothers but actually fulfills their highest intentions and dreams.

God *is* Love, and love in varied forms — nurture, support, provision, tenderness, playfulness — is the substance of the mother/child experience. Even though our babies may at times provoke negative personal feelings, the context in which these feelings arise continually invites us to find ways to overcome them and to discover and promote the best in ourselves and our children.

Most books for parents are about children: how to take care of and manage children at various ages and stages. A few others recognize the stress and difficulty of parenthood and offer sympathy and "survival" tips. The implication is that parenthood is a service done to and for children at considerable cost to the parents, who legitimately resent the demands even though volunteering for the duty. Yet becoming a parent is so crucial to large numbers of people that infertility is a major field of medical technology in our day. This phenomenon would seem to confirm that what people are really seeking, in their pursuit of babies, is precisely the participation in and expression of the God qualities that parenthood allows. However we may think of it personally, we all want to be bigger and better than what we seem to be as solitary persons.

Motherhood Offers What It Requires:
The Discovery of Love as a Law

If we think motherhood is just a matter of "having" or "getting" a baby that we then "raise" as best we can out of our personal resources, our vision of what we are about is obscured by the lens of personal beliefs that keeps our seeing restricted. Our motherhood, in this case, tends to be largely a rerun of our mother's motherhood, for good or ill. I recently read a letter to an advice columnist in which a young mother begged for help. She found herself treating her beautiful young son just as badly as she had been treated, and she was desperate to find some way to avoid hurting him as she had been hurt. *Parental mentality repeats in the children unless and until we find a base from which to call it into question. The only base sufficient to release the pictures of a personal past is that of the Divine.*

Seeing motherhood as a personal project, we often feel inadequate or anxious. The sense of demand and responsibility attendant upon a personal view of motherhood is so unbearable that we often feel driven beyond personal resources. The spiritual fact underlying this human experience is that we are being invited, again and again, to discover that Life is *not* personal and that its universal law is Love. It is because Life is an already established substance of qualities rather than an unpredictable series of personal interactions that we can feel Its reliable goodness. And without being able to feel the reliability of good, we can never feel Love as absolutely real.

Motherhood, from conception on, is a continuing stretch beyond the mother's old, limited human identity beliefs. That's both the crisis and the marvel of it. It is unfortunately true that most of us do not seek beyond the narrowest horizon unless and until we are forced to do so. We want our lives to be dynamic and expanding but find new experiences difficult, nonetheless. At base, the issue is always fear. The new is unknown, and the unknown is always frightening to personal ego sense.

The anxiety that a new mother experiences may result in a basically adversarial mentality asserting itself in relation to the baby. A single mother, particularly, lacking the reassuring presence of another adult and another perspective on things, may unwittingly think of the baby as a potential threat to her own life and well-being, however desperately she wanted to have a child. In fact, the greater a woman's difficulty in becoming a mother, the greater the likelihood of an underlying fear of it, which often turns into hostility toward the baby. Until this point, the woman seemed to be in control of her life and her affairs. But from the moment the baby arrives, it is clear that this other little life, which so impacts her own, is not under her personal control, and this can feel threatening. It is important to find a framework of thinking that adds another dimension to the antagonistic self/other perspective, and only God provides this.

Entertaining an Angel

In order to make the divine Presence more tangible, particularly in moments of crisis, it may be useful to think of

it as an angel. We could truthfully say that a baby doesn't
come into our home alone ... it brings an angel along with
it. So we are never alone with a baby. There are always
mother, child, and angel. This angel is the angel of Love,
and it is present to serve both mother and infant. "And he
shall give his angels charge over thee, to keep thee in all
thy ways," says Psalm 91. This angel Presence loves, nurtures, supports, and guides the mother as much as it loves,
nurtures, and supports the baby. When a mother finds herself thinking negative thoughts about the baby, resenting
it, complaining about it, or fearfully fantasizing what the
child might become, she can remind herself that the angel
is present, having charge over both herself and the baby,
to keep them both in Goodness in all aspects of their experience. She doesn't have to anticipate what may go wrong
with her child and try to prevent it.

Just Like Our Kids, We Grow from Stage to Stage

The discoveries made at each stage of motherhood prepare
the mother for the next stage, just as the child's mastery of
each level's developmental skills or tasks prepares him for
the next. However much our personal sense may protest
having to stretch and yield, the gifts of growth are worth as
much to us as our child's development is to him. Watching
our babies and toddlers rushing to meet each new developmental task, impelled from within and undaunted by the
bumps and falls along the way, provides us with inspiration
for our own development. When the gifts of one stage are
refused or ignored, the next stage seems even more difficult.
But Life lets us play "catch-up" at any point. Any discovery
of truth that we make at any point blesses us and our children immediately and actually tends to undo the seeming
consequences of past mistakes.

"If Momma Ain't Happy, Ain't Nobody Happy," But if Momma Is Happy . . .

Motherhood involves a great deal of busyness, and many women unwittingly fall for the belief that it is by busyness that they prove their worth to their husbands and children, and especially to themselves. The flip side of this belief is the sense of having no time for oneself, of being a martyr to the needs of the family. I made a wonderful discovery, early on, with my husband's help. One morning, when the children were very little and I had a class to teach that evening, I felt very sorry for myself. I sat holding the baby, with my toddler by my side, and cried. The content of my misery was some variation on the theme of being overwhelmed by demands, since this was my chronic, human sense of things. Jan, my husband, came into the room. I hoped for some sympathy, some concern. Instead, he sat down and said, kindly but firmly, "You've got to get happy. I don't care what it takes: quit work, get a sitter, whatever. But you've got to get happy, because the whole family suffers when you cry like this."

After he left for work, I thought about what he had said. My human desire to defend my pitiable situation was overridden by the truthfulness of his comments. I hated the thought of my little boys being dragged down by a crying mother. At that moment, I saw clearly that my first and foremost responsibility was to find resources for myself, to find the foundation for peace and joy. None of what I was doing for the family would be any good if I could not provide a mental climate of happiness. I saw that the mother's consciousness is the center of the home, *is* the home, since "home" is clearly a state of consciousness rather than a place. So if mother is happy, then everyone in the home is blessed by her happiness. This is not a burden, but a privilege and a place of dominion.

The spiritual dimension in thinking always expands, heals, and unifies. The "findings" and "gettings" of home and husband and child are unfoldments in consciousness first of all. Thirty years ago I was convinced that I would never find a husband, never have a home, never be a mother. Working consciously to understand Life spiritually, I found the personal beliefs that were blocking the unfoldment of these desirable human situations unmasked and dissolved. Then marriage, home, and children could appear as my experience. And then of course I discovered, as we all do, that when one's longed-for situations do appear, they are not happy endings but challenging beginnings.

New motherhood is entrance into the best school for Love-awareness that I know of. There is nothing to fear but much to be gratefully discovered. In his famous Sermon on the Mount (Luke 12:31–32) Jesus advises his listeners not to worry about the details of personal life, but to "seek ... the kingdom of God; and all these things shall be added unto you." This teaching is of the greatest practical value to mothers. Jesus is not just being poetic here. He is telling us exactly how Life works and how our needs get met.

We may understand the kingdom of God to be the conscious awareness of Life as divine qualities. When we continually and consciously acknowledge that God's quality Life is what is really going on, right where we are, we open the field of our human activities to the dynamic energy of that divine Life. This is how we let God raise our children. The "all things" that get "added" include the health and well-being of our family. And, lest we think that we are personally responsible to seek the right mental state for God to do his work, Jesus concludes, "Fear not, little flock, for it is your Father's good pleasure to give you the kingdom." Thus are we promised that we will be raised, in consciousness, in light and truth, as well as our children.

Motherhood's Social Significance

Because quality Life is the foundation of all positive social structures and change, there is a larger, cultural value to motherhood. The role itself is a metaphor for an enabling, nurturing mentality. A society that values and celebrates the loving qualities inherent in the mother/child relationship is oriented toward unity, support, affection, and spontaneity. A society that celebrates separate-person success, sometimes at the cost of another's welfare, is unwittingly inviting adversarialness and even violence.

We are just pulling out of an unfortunate period during which motherhood has been denigrated in favor of personal achievement. During this period, aggressive interpersonal qualities have developed dominance in the public thinking. We are inundated with images of horror and violence that are valued as entertainment even though decried as experience. Perhaps the most stunning evidence of this distortion of values occurred at the time of the mobilization of the military to meet the crisis in the Persian Gulf. A number of magazines featured photos of women in full battle dress, saying goodbye to their children, even newborn babies. When warrior qualities are promoted as higher and more important than the mothering of infants, a culture is in trouble. True feminism has lost out when a woman considers herself more valuable as a soldier than as a mother.

In a sense, every mother mothers "for God" as well as for her children and herself. She is an expression in the world of the Godly values and energies that heal and harmonize the discordant human mentality. Understanding this, no mother ever needs to feel less valuable than women who work and achieve outside the home. The value of activity, wherever it takes place, lies in the consciousness of the individual and the qualities that motivate and manifest in the activity. We are not here for personal gratification nor for the gratification of our children. We are here for the Love-awareness that blesses us, our children, and the world.

▪

MOTHER'S RESOURCE GUIDE for Chapter 1

Some Things To Do

Your first priority as a mother is to find resources for your own peace and joy and assurance. Your happiness assures the baby's well-being; your unhappiness casts a pall over the whole family.

Make sure you take time for whatever reading, meditation, prayer, or guidance you need to keep mentally on track. Throughout my entire twenty years of active mothering, I always dialogued regularly with a spiritual teacher. The teachers varied over the years, but I have always been grateful for this ongoing guidance. In addition, I have always found fresh, inspiring written material coming my way.

The Bible is the book of our spiritual roots, no matter what our current religious position. When we learn to read it from a spiritual standpoint, we find it to be an ever-fresh well of inspiration and support. *The Runner's Bible* by Nora Holm offers brief texts with some commentary, arranged under specific topics that address needs such a fearfulness, lack, insecurity, etc. The little book is invaluable and children enjoy using it on their own, once they can read.

Physical exercise is valuable for its mental as well as physical benefits. Walking is particularly appropriate because it releases consciousness rather than captivating it. I like to walk in parks, where the views are refreshing. When my mind is muddled or busy, a walk will quiet thoughts, clarify issues, and invigorate me physically and mentally.

Be good to yourself in consciousness. Let yourself feast on the lovely views of Spirit, and consciousness will bless you and raise your children in beauty and health.

Meditations

"BE HAPPY, MOTHER..."

Happiness leaves nothing undone. If you are happy, you cannot fail to hear the Song of God. If you are happy, you have no interest in darkening your mind with grievances against anyone, and so you are naturally kind and consistently fair. And how could you not be free of the world's countless addictions if within you felt a deep contentment?... Can joy and peace ever be out of place?... And so, by being happy, you are all you ever need be: loving, just, pure, and compassionate. And your every step is guided and blessed by the Song of God.[1]

THE TWENTY-THIRD PSALM
Commentary by Ann Tremaine Linthorst

The Lord is my shepherd
   I am guided from within by divine Love/Intelligence.
I shall not want
   My needs — material, emotional, mental, spiritual —
   are ever met.
He maketh me to lie down in green pastures
   Peace, rest, abundant goodness surround me.
He leadeth me beside the still waters
   Deep, tranquil confidence is mine.
He restoreth my soul
   I am renewed with fresh springs of vitality and joy.

He leadeth me in the paths of righteousness for his name's sake

I am guided to right understanding and spiritual growth, so that my presence may bear witness to divine Love.

Yea, though I walk through the valley of the shadow of death, I will fear no evil, for thou art with me

Even when things seem most desperate, I will remember that God — goodness — is the Reality of things.

Thy rod and thy staff, they comfort me

The spiritual laws of Life are always operating. I can lean on them as I lean on the buoyancy of water.

Thou preparest a table before me in the presence of mine enemies

God is the source of my supply, and no human can interfere with it.

Thou anointest my head with oil; my cup runneth over

My identity, worth, and fullness of being are bestowed by God and are always available to me.

Surely goodness and mercy shall follow me all the days of my life,

and I will dwell in the house of the Lord forever

I am confident that my life is the unfoldment of good and that my destiny is to live in the consciousness of Love forever.

Recommended Reading

Berends, Polly. *Whole Child/Whole Parent.* New York: Harper & Row, 1983.

Chapter 2

INFANCY
The Crisis of Personal Identity /
The Marvel of Spiritual Identity

WHO IS THE MOTHER HERE?

For the first few weeks after I brought the baby home, I noticed the same, insistent thought recurring in consciousness: "I'm not a mother. I've just got this little baby hanging around my house all the time."

The first baby is a crisis for both parents, no matter who they are or how prepared they may be. My conscious fears, ahead of time, focused on not knowing what to do. So, I made a point of choosing rooming-in at the hospital. The babies were kept at the mothers' bedsides during the day, and the nurses showed us the basics of physical care. It turned out when I got the baby home that the details of physical care pretty well took care of themselves.

The real crisis presented itself to me in the insistent thought that I was not yet a mother even though the baby was there. I'm apparently not the first new parent to have such a thought. A comic strip called "Baby Blues" shows a new father saying, "I can't believe this all happened so fast. First, the pregnancy, then the birth, and now we're a family. I'm not ready! I'm not prepared! I'm a premature father!"

This is exactly the crisis. The baby's arrival turns us into mothers overnight, but the identity "mother" does not arrive so instantly. My friend Chris, whose first baby arrived a month late, reported: "I just wasn't myself for months after his birth." She had no idea why she felt this way and no tools for resolving it. But she certainly stated the issue clearly. One is now called "mother," but "mother" is not oneself! The new identity just doesn't match up yet and may leave a woman feeling like she doesn't know who she is. Like most women, Chris just muddled on, and the confused sense eventually passed. But it is so much easier when we know what's going on and can work directly to resolve it.

The Universal Crisis of Being a Mother

Crises are always "in here" — in consciousness — and not "out there" in persons, places, or things. It is what having a baby means to one's mental pictures of oneself and one's life, and the emotional turmoil arising out of that meaning, which constitute a crisis. When a woman fantasizes about having a baby, it is done from the vantage point of a non-mother, and she thinks of her independent, individual self having a fun, cute little object around to love and fuss with. But when she brings this little one home, her whole life is irrevocably changed in unimaginable ways. Nothing is the same. Her marriage is shaken up, her personal freedom of movement is non-existent, everything in her life revolves around the care of a small, cranky stranger. Of course, we don't begin to register, at the beginning, all of the profound changes that a child brings into our experience. But becoming "mother" is, itself, a big change. It is understandable that such a substantial identity shift causes anxiety and takes some getting used to.

This is the universal crisis of becoming a mother, the one that every woman goes through with her first child. If we think about the other "firsts" of our experience, we realize that any new experience produces anxiety. So we shouldn't be surprised about being anxious as new mothers and feeling inadequate to the task. Such questions as "How do I know what to do?" "Will I be a good mother?" "Will I do something wrong and damage the baby?" are to be expected.

The Peril of Possessive Thinking

How we think about becoming a mother before the baby arrives makes a difference in our post-partum experience. When we think about getting pregnant or adopting, we need to ask ourselves, "Do I want to be a mother?" and not just, "Would I like to have a baby?" The two questions are not the same, and we need to see the difference. The desire for a baby is often a possessive fantasy that arises out of a woman's pre-maternal sense. She wants to get something for herself, and such a desire is bound to disappoint. Long before I became a mother, I loved Gibran's treatise on children:

> Your children are not your children.
> They are the sons and daughters of Life's longing for itself.
> They come through you but not from you,
> And though they are with you yet they belong not to you.[2]

A possessive idea of having a baby quickly bankrupts — proves itself misguided — by the problems that arise from it. One graphic example is the mother who wanted a baby of one sex so badly that she couldn't even bear the thought of bringing home her newborn of the opposite sex. *When we want something for ourselves, the self's specifications may become so narrow that they obscure from us the goodness of what we have.* On the other hand, if a woman wants to become a mother, then she is already oriented to new experiences. Equipped with a spiritual viewpoint, the new mother's mentality is one of looking to see what Life is revealing of its nature and lawfulness rather than deciding personally what she wants and then demanding Life to produce it.

Dr. Spock's Dilemma

While there is a lot of information available to a pregnant or adopting woman in terms of learning about babies and child care, there is little attention paid to her need to be preparing mentally for a new identity. Moreover, the support and guidance in terms of child care can be troublesome as well as helpful. We are too self-conscious about the whole thing, largely because so much has been written about the psychological issues of mothering.

A few years ago, I heard Dr. Spock speak, and he confessed to having unwittingly opened a Pandora's box with his book on child care. What started out as a simple desire to help parents respond constructively to the common problems arising in infancy and early childhood ended up making parents fearful of damaging their children emotionally. The very parents who educated themselves in order to be better parents became, Spock found, immobilized by fear of doing the wrong thing. They distrusted their natural responses. He reported that in a group of a dozen families being followed by a hospital research team, the only one that had no problems with toilet training was the uneducated couple who had not read his book! And he found that, even though he spoke with the others and urged them to go with their own natural sense of what was best, they were unable to do so.

This illustrates to me that the need in parent education is for education in the highest understanding of motherhood and fatherhood rather than on "doing" things to or for or with the child. There is not a single right way to schedule, feed, cuddle, or otherwise handle the baby. The most important issue for the baby is the state of the mother's consciousness. *The mother's first priority is her own mental health and happiness, because the mother's consciousness constitutes the baby's world.* This may seem to put even more pressure on the mother to "do it right" mentally, but actually it is the secret of the mother's dominion. We cannot control a little baby out there, but we can find resources for health and peace within our own thinking.

Motherhood Is the Universe of Love Expressing Itself

Motherhood is first of all the opening out of the mother's mental horizons, an expansion of her identity, her environment, her whole sense of herself and life. There is a universe to be discovered of greater Love and Good than she has ever known. In fact, the conception or adoption of a baby *is* that universe of Love, which has always been the truth of our lives, expressing itself in greater fullness. It helps dispel the burdensome belief in personal responsibility if we see that we are becoming mothers because the qualities that are the essence of motherhood are already the substance of our knowing and being. *Each new mother is not called upon to reinvent motherhood from scratch. Mother/child qualities are already ours or we would never be interested in becoming mothers in the first place.* As new mothers we are just discovering these incredibly positive and significant truths about reality more fully. But Life is doing the whole show; we are just along for the ride, that is, for the conscious awareness of it.

Having been single for many years and having despaired of ever marrying and having children, I was particularly conscious of the first months of motherhood as a privileged time. I had heard many mothers of older children comment that the early years were "the best time" and I was determined to enjoy these years. I was a very new spiritual student at that time and understood little, but I did know that the quality of my experience was a matter of the state of my consciousness rather than of external events.

We lived in a New York City apartment at the time, and when the weather was good, the mothers of infants and toddlers tended to congregate with their offspring around a flagpole in the center of the complex. I noticed that the conversation was a sort of "Can you top this?" of complaints. "My baby cried all night...." "Well, my son didn't sleep through the night until he was three years old!..." "Susie, here, has had an ear infection for months...." "Well, Billy has had so much penicillin he had an allergic reaction...." and on and on. It is entirely understandable: there is comfort in knowing that others are going through the horrors that you are experiencing — then they don't seem so horrible. But I hoped for something better than shared horrors. I wanted to experience the actual goodness of "the best time." I was determined not to let a litany of complaints dominate my thinking until the kids were grown and then look back with nostalgia and say, "It was best when they were little."

So I made a point of holding to my own private mental agenda of noticing and enjoying everything I could about my new situation. If our viewpoint is limited to what our personal identity sense reports to us, these years of full-time care of infants and small children can seem to be the pits. For me, knowing that every situation could point me to clearer seeing of the ultimate goodness of Life provided the boost I needed to really enjoy this time. *Marvels tend not to show themselves uninvited. A conscious desire to see beyond the crises and a willingness to do the mental work required constitute the invitation that bears marvelous fruits.* I was aware of the contrast between my sense of my situation and that of a friend in the apartment house who had two children similarly separated in age. When I discovered I was pregnant with our second baby, I mentioned it to her and said, "Tell me honestly, Marsha, how is it to have two kids sixteen months apart?" Without a moment's hesitation, she exclaimed, "It's just horrible!" But I'll bet that she is now looking back and remembering those years as "the best time of all."

The False Beliefs Underlying a Mother's Performance Anxieties

The new mother's performance anxieties reflect not simply a lack of information, but a false belief: "Because this baby is here, I am supposed to be a full-fledged, graduate Mother, knowing how to handle anything that may come up." This belief is outrageous and needs to be challenged directly. Is that the way Life is? Do we, enrolling our children in kindergarten, expect them to already know what they will know when they graduate from high school? Of course not. Well, then, we can assume that it is not required of us either. The baby and the mother are a team. Each is perfectly equipped to provide the other with what is needed. The baby gives the mother the opportunity to let motherhood qualities unfold themselves, and the mother spontaneously gives the baby what he or she needs. First babies are for the training of the parents and first parents are for the marveling over of new babies, and it actually works very well.

A Mother's Personal Problems

Sometimes, however, the identity crisis is complicated by already present personal problems of the mother. Our mental picture of "mother" is, as mentioned, determined first of all by our own mothers. When a woman's childhood experience was one of poor or absent mothering, then donning the cloak of mother identity is especially problematic. The sense of unfinished work around the mother/child issue continues, and her own mental picture of being a needy child remains a significant identity factor. That picture has its own agenda: to get the mothering not provided or redo the negative experience in order to reverse "the damage."

For such a woman, becoming a mother constitutes a threat to the self that sees itself inadequately mothered. She seems required now to be the caregiver, to be responsible for nurturing, supporting, and loving the baby. To her picture of herself as a little starved or abused child needing nurture, that looms like an overwhelming and unmeetable demand. "I didn't get enough myself! I still want to be taken care of myself! How can I possibly give love and care to my baby?"

Moreover, there is a strange belief that one's opportunity to be mothered somehow ends with becoming a mother oneself. It seems as if Life is saying, "Okay, your chance is over. You've gotten all you are going to get. Now you are the giver and not the receiver of support and nurture." This is perhaps the most traumatic false belief surrounding new motherhood. It is absolute nonsense. Quite the opposite is true. Nonetheless, this belief that motherhood closes the door to being nurtured and cared for is troublesome. I think it is a factor in two major problems: an inability to conceive, in the first place, and post-partum depression. Both these problems reflect some difficulty in accepting the identity of mother, because of what it seems to mean to the woman's self-image. In the extreme cases of post-partum psychosis, where a baby is harmed, it is not a lack of love for the baby, but the sense of having to reject mother-identity absolutely, that is the issue. The baby's presence, representing the sense of an unmeetable demand or an unbearable deprivation, cannot be tolerated.

When a woman's belief about herself and motherhood are this obscuring, special treatment is needed. Help is available on many levels and in many ways. No matter what the form or language in which the help comes, however, the healing of the false mentality can only come about by the truth of Being asserting itself over the unbearable lies of personal sense. The familiar theological idea that God is omnipresent becomes of utmost practicality as the truth that God is already present, doing and being the loving and the nurturing and the guiding of both mother and baby. Nobody is asking a mother to be her child's god.

Freedom from Invisible Family Heirlooms

The identity of "mother" has the specific positive and negative meanings of our own mother's sense of motherhood. We are all subject to invisible family heirlooms, handed down through the generations, from mother, and sometimes father, to daughter. These family beliefs masquerade as our feelings and our thinking, and we assume that they must be ours simply because we seem to feel and think that way. But they are not ours in any legitimate sense. We did not create them and would not choose them, so why should we suffer from their claims on our consciousness? And even more to the point, why should we let our children become the targets of this family garbage?

One of Jesus' most profound and transforming teachings is the injunction in Matthew 23:9 to "call no man your father upon the earth; for one is your Father, which is in heaven." This applies to "mother" as well. This single sentence contains the liberation of us and of our children from the invisible family heirlooms of false identity. We are to look to God alone as the Source of our identities. On this basis, we call into question the feelings that arise in response to our babies and trace the feelings back to the underlying beliefs.

We can develop a habit of thought in the very beginning that can help us at every stage of our children's development. *When we find ourselves feeling anxious or negative about the child's behavior, we ask ourselves: "What is my problem here? What belief about things is making me uncomfortable?"* This gives us the chance to let our old beliefs surface, so that they may be identified as old beliefs and not projected blindly onto the baby. Seeing this, instead of becoming angry at the child, we can consciously separate the feelings from the child and seek the spiritual truth that can heal the mistaken beliefs.

Carolyn, for example, found herself interpreting her baby's fussing as "whining" or "grumpiness" and thus became aware that "being grumpy" was the cardinal sin in her mother's eyes. Discovering this old family motto — "We're not getting grumpy, are we?" — arising every time the baby made a certain kind of sound enabled Carolyn to unhook from the family heirloom. She was then able to seek to understand the baby's communication and even respond and reply to it rather than labeling it unacceptable and feeling a pressure to stop or prevent it.

Julie, on the other hand, found herself interpreting her baby's whimpers as a sign of illness. Her first thought was, "Is she sick?" and she was immediately fearful. Julie had grown up in a mental climate of fearful preoccupation with physical symptoms. At first she felt driven to call the doctor at the baby's every cry. But when she learned to investigate her own thinking first, she was able to spot her family heirloom at work. She could then work on her own fearfulness by seeking a spiritual sense of Life. As she became more confident, Julie began to enjoy the baby's presence and verbalizations rather than fear them.

Baby's Illnesses Reflect
Parental Stress and Anxiety

Seeing motherhood as a spiritual journey does not impose some belief system upon motherhood but enables us to remove the imposed personal beliefs that give rise to the problems of human motherhood. Knowing that negative experiences are not the fruits of Life's true nature gives us the standpoint from which we can call into question the stresses and illnesses that are the common experience of mothers and new babies. I feel certain that most of the ordinary physical ailments of the baby's first year — colic, ear and throat infections, and fevers — are a reflection of the parents' anxieties and stress. Knowing this brings our attention back to issues of our own consciousness.

One of the hardest parts of motherhood is being confronted with a sick baby, especially in the middle of the night. We feel so frightened and helpless. It is important and reassuring to have an established procedure for getting help in time of emergency. For me this meant having a sympathetic and capable pediatrician for the kids and a spiritual guide for myself. Sometimes I was able to resolve the illness in consciousness, without needing to go to the doctor. At times I gratefully asked for help from a Christian Science Practitioner. But if I felt at all concerned or uncertain, I went, with equal gratitude, to the doctor. I am all for working things out spiritually, if one is spiritually advanced enough to do so. But parents need to be free to use every help available without feeling guilty or inadequate for doing so. Polly Berends wisely commented, "We do what we have to do while seeking to know what we need to know."

Doing whatever we need to do to assure ourselves of the baby's well-being allows us then to deal with the basic problem, which is fear. *The fear doesn't come from the baby's illness;*

rather, the illness comes from the fear. Both the illness and the fear arise from the belief that we are alone and without the support of some reliable and ever-present Goodness. The need, then, is to discover that supporting Good. The more I was able to deal with my anxieties by becoming conscious of the presence of Love, the less severe were the boys' illnesses and the less frequent were visits to the doctor.

The Crisis of a Screaming Baby

An infant's crying is a powerful trigger to personal issue in the consciousness of the one who is caring for it. Most infant abuse, I suspect, is in reaction to crying that cannot be stopped. In every case, it is what the uncontrollable crying means to the mother that drives her to desperation. If she can be alert to her thinking at such a moment, she will find that not being able to quiet the baby makes her feel threatened in some unbearable way. The issue is always fear and the attempt to quiet the baby arises out of the mother's survival sense. She feels *she* is in danger if the baby cannot be quieted.

One new mother discovered that the intensity and pitch of her infant's cry made her feel like she was being stabbed by a sharp knife. She couldn't tolerate the sound for more than a few minutes. This ingenious mother found that using ear plugs muffled the sound sufficiently to relieve her distress. Seeing her feelings as her problem rather than the baby's, she then found a simple solution.

Sometimes prolonged crying is interpreted as criticism of the mother. A new mother, particularly, may feel that if she was doing her job right, the baby would not cry. In such a case, the poor baby is not permitted to have and voice any issues of its own because they trigger self-recrimination and blame in the mother's thinking.

Discovering That We Can't Go Wrong

The first step in all problem solving is owning the problem. Our babies are not doing something bad to us. Our feelings of desperation are a consequence of beliefs and pressures in our consciousness. With the first baby, those pressures almost always involve a fear that we will be inadequate and will fail as mother. What every new mother needs to know is that she can't go wrong, as long as she keeps acknowledging the baby's spiritual Source and quality identity. When she does this she is letting God, rather than family garbage, raise the baby. We don't have to prohibit or punish infant behavior, but simply to rejoice in the truth of divine Life. Relieved of the terror of personal responsibility to "do" the baby right, the new mother can begin to relax and enjoy her baby.

Motherhood is not a personal performance and a baby is not a personal project. We and our babies already possess the qualities of perfect Life, and we are together to enhance and potentiate the unfoldment of each one's quality identity. It is important that we regularly take time to remind ourselves of the spiritual facts of Being. Starting from the divine standpoint in thinking before personal sense has a chance to stir up a crisis works a lot better than waiting until we feel fearful and stressed. When we start out mindful of Life as already full and good, we are less likely to be taken in completely by the mental pictures of personhood.

Looking to See Spirit

No matter what seems to be going on, personally and interpersonally, it does not change the substance of spiritual reality. Just as the matrix of natural law that governs our physical universe remains untouched by interpersonal events, so the universe of Spirit remains intact at all times. Any room we are in is actually filled with the qualities of Life: love, intelligence, harmony, order, beauty, innocence, peace. When I was anxious about a baby's crying, I would sometimes say, out loud, "Peace is here, filling this room. Love is here, filling this room. Harmony is here, filling this room." This helped me be aware of being surrounded by this higher Presence, even if I couldn't personally feel those things at that moment.

No situation is ever going to give us the qualities of Good. The desperation that a mother can feel when trying to make a baby be quiet so that she can find some peace is a consequence of coming at the issue from the wrong end. The Bible speaks of "the peace that passeth understanding." This is the peace that exists despite the noise of the human scene, the peace that reflects the wholeness and rightness of God's quality Life. A quiet baby cannot give us peace, but the consciousness of peace can give us a quiet baby.

"God Helps Those Who Let Him"

We don't have to — and can't — personally solve our personal problems. This is because the real problem is looking at our situation from a personal standpoint. We need to come at the seeming problem from a higher viewpoint. "God helps those who let Him," says Thomas Hora. We let God help us by shifting from personal thinking to quality awareness.

The following dialogue took place between a "young mother who had considerable difficulties with her children..." and the spiritually oriented psychiatrist to whom she went "to find out how to handle her family."

She was told, "Look here, if the faucet in your kitchen is acting up, then you fix it, right? But if your children are acting up, you can't fix them. Somebody else has to fix them."

"That's why I am going to a psychiatrist," the mother replied.

"But the psychiatrist cannot fix them either. A psychiatrist is not a plumber of little children. Somebody else has to fix them."

"Well, who then?"

"Well, God has to fix them."

The patient exclaimed, "God! There is no God in our house." But she learned that God could be invited into the house, provided she saw to it that the house had a loving climate. And this loving climate had to come through her consciousness, through her ways of thinking and viewing life. The first good thing that came of this was that she stopped trying to handle her children.... Then she started to work it out with God, and one day, she said, "You know, Doctor, it works so well that I suspect it's a gimmick."[3]

Having invited God into the house, we have more time and energy available to gratefully enjoy Life's show. It is amazing to watch the infant's growth, the ordered unfoldment of physical and mental attributes that we not only don't have to make happen but cannot prevent, even by our clumsy new mothering. It is much more enriching to celebrate the baby's growth as Life's blooming than to take it as grounds for personal bragging. *Parents who want personal credit for their baby's development have missed out on the biggest marvel of new parenthood: the God-givenness of the good that so relieves the hell of personal responsibility.* And they have set themselves up for the burdens of false godhood, thinking they have to make their kids be smart and good and feeling personally discredited if problems arise.

Mothering One's Child Is Self-Mothering

Though it may take the new mother some time to realize it, motherhood is not the end of feeling mothered. Rather, one discovers that mothering one's child is self-mothering. Giving and getting become one for mother and baby. Looking back I can see that having children gave me permission to be a kid in so many ways, at the same time that I enjoyed the added dimension of motherhood, which does have its privileges as well as its problems. And I found my children, even when very small, mothering me at times. Motherness/ childness is a package — wherever you come into it, the whole is there.

Couple Discomforts Are Not Marital Problems

Even when all goes well, the arrival of the first child changes radically and permanently the parents' identities and life-style. And, again, however much this change and expansion has been sought, it does not come easily to personal sense. The father has his own issues of identity, and each parent's identity discomforts impact on the other, so that couples often experience a good deal of strain in their relationship until the individual crises are resolved. The new mother often turns to her husband for additional help and support, both emotionally and physically. Fortunately, many couples today more fully share the tasks and emotional stresses of parenthood. But new fathers sometimes feel quite bereft of wifely support and affection, as the woman shifts her attention and energy to the baby.

It is good to know that such feelings and changes in the relationship are not marital problems. These are issues of growth and expansion for each individual, and growth can only make the marriage stronger and more mature.

For the father as for the mother, the need is to be alert to the marvels that the expanding awareness discovers rather than hunkering down to try to keep the old sense of things comfortable.

The Immediacy of the Marvels

Despite the newness and scariness of the first days, the marvels are immediately in evidence. My first conscious discovery occurred in the hospital, the first time I stood at the nursery window and saw my baby among the others. His face was riveting to me; I felt an absolute identification with that little face that surprised me. My husband felt it too. He said, "When the other babies cry, I think it's cute. But when I see Tommy crying, I can't stand it." I was amazed to notice how the baby evokes from the world into which it comes the very things it needs. The baby is such a graphic picture of child qualities that the corresponding nurturing, protecting parent qualities arise spontaneously. A psychologist once explained to me that a mother and her newborn have a symbiotic mental attachment. This means that they are one consciousness. It is just what the newborn needs. I blush, now, to think of how shamelessly preoccupied with this first baby I was: how I babbled on, assuming that everyone was as enamored with him as I; how I, the most modest of women, breast-fed him in groups of friends completely without self-consciousness.

Finding mother qualities so immediately evoked in myself and even in my husband was the beginning of the overall discovery of the marvelous fact that *motherhood is not a personal task and a personal responsibility. It is the spiritual facts of Being coming more clearly to light. What the mother really needs to fulfill her role is to be present to the baby, not only physically, but mentally. We do that primarily by noticing what is happening.*

Feeling personally responsible to do everything right makes us feel anxious, and this anxiety screens out our awareness of the very evidence of a larger Good that can relieve the anxiety. So it is important to remind ourselves that the anxiety is the problem, not the baby, and that the anxiety is a sign of some false belief imposing itself on our thinking. What is going on here is good, and we have nothing to fear from paying attention. One of the keys to being able to notice the marvels of new motherhood and of the newborn baby is mental preparation. I wanted to know everything I could about newborns before I was left alone with one, and I found out some basic facts that were enormously reassuring.

The main thing I learned from my reading was that, while newborns may appear very fragile and helpless, they are in many ways very tough. They are little growth machines, designed at this point to screen out most external stimuli so that all their energies can be devoted to the big, beginning task of growing on their own, apart from the mother's body. The mother really has very little to do except watch over this little Life expression. Keeping the baby fed, dry, clean, comfortable, and cuddled, while he or she gets on with growing, is all we can and need to do.

The fear that something more, something enormous and impossible, is demanded of us only works to hide the simplicity of the task with newborns. A rocking chair is probably the only essential piece of equipment for the mother. Just sitting in it with the baby in her arms works wonders. I found fragments of the songs my mother sang to me coming to mind, and before I knew it, I was rocking and singing and feeling like a mother after all. "So lula, lula, lula, lula, bye-bye. Does ya want the moon to play with, and the stars to run away with? They'll come if you don't cry." In singing to my baby the same precious melodies my mother sang to me, I became loved child as well as loving mother, my baby and I the loved and lovely and loving illustration of Love divine. For the mother whose own mother never sang to her, singing to the baby means Mother-Love singing to her as well, healing the hurt, filling the seeming void in her own experience.

Our Babies Show Us That Life Is Doing Itself Through and As Us

Of course, for the first few weeks, we may find it hard to believe that we don't have to keep the baby breathing and eating. We check every few minutes to make sure that everything is happening as it should. But then we begin to relax and notice how it is all unfolding from within, according to some inner timetable of its own. The baby eats, sleeps, smiles, then — suddenly, miraculously — turns over, sits up, sprouts teeth and hair. The child's first year is the most dramatic period of physical growth in the whole life span. It is the clearest expression we shall see in the child's development of the ultimate truth of things: that Life does Itself through and as us. Life is found to be an already-fullness of qualities that is eternally busy about expressing Itself in an infinite variety of forms.

This discovery encompasses the whole of our experience and has ramifications far beyond child care. It is the absolute denial of the human misconception of things, which is that we have to "do" what we call "our own" or "our children's" lives: make them good and prevent them from being bad. This human, doing perspective makes parenthood a very mixed blessing.

Until parenthood, humans may fool themselves that they are in charge of their lives, running the show. Personal achievement and personal gratification are central values of upwardly mobile individuals or couples. Even marriage may seem to be something that one can personally orchestrate, and when this proves impossible, one can keep the pretense going by blaming the spouse. But parenthood is another matter.

Conception Is an Issue of Consciousness

One cannot successfully "do" a child, from conception on. With all due respect to the technological wonders of reproductive engineering, conception is an issue of consciousness. When problems in consciousness are not resolved, the attempt to force pregnancy technologically, though many times successful, may exact a terrible price in physical, emotional, interpersonal, and financial suffering.

This does not mean that we may not use any and every available form of aid, if needed, to become pregnant. But it does mean that we recognize there is a mental obstacle involved that needs to be dissolved by spiritual understanding. Getting the baby is just the start, and the personal beliefs that cause us problems in conception and delivery will continue to show up. But each difficulty is an opportunity to make liberating discoveries about Life. Technology is not the problem but the limited viewpoint that sees life to be material and thus something to be personally engineered.

Motherhood is most likely to unfold and to be positive when we understand that, with or without children, Life is divine and therefore complete. The less we look to any detail of personal experience as a requirement for our happiness, the more certain and unprecarious our happiness is. We learn to find fulfillment in the awareness of Life's qualities as already ours. Establishing the Good in consciousness first, we find that divine Good unfolding effortlessly in appropriate forms. Feeling filled by Life, we can be lovingly present to our babies.

Love Is Seeing the Child's Quality Identity

In her unique and illuminating book *Whole Child/Whole Parent*, Polly Berends describes the kind of seeing that makes motherhood marvelous and that is actually the purest expression of love. She writes:

> The baby is dirty all the time. We are constantly changing his diapers and wiping his bottom. And yet it is so easy to see that he is pure.... We are not at all deceived by the mess into thinking that he is either impure or stupid.
>
> This purity we see — that's the truth! And the distinguishing we do between the purity and the mess, that's love! ... Love is not the diaper changing or the fixing of meals or disciplining or whatever it is that we must do along the way. *Love is the sorting out in thought* of the perfect child from all suggestions to the contrary.[4]

We could also say that "Love is the sorting out in thought of the child's quality identity from all the misconceptions of personhood." The most important thing we do for our children is to see them as already possessing the qualities of Good. We can do this if and only if we look at them as God's children rather than the offspring of our personal identities. Getting this clear at the beginning puts us on a foundation of assurance for dealing with everything that comes up from then on.

We are good and our children are good not because we or they try to be good persons, but because Life is made up of good qualities. We never have to try to operate upon our children to make them be good or make them not be bad. They are here to discover their quality identities, and we have the privilege and joy of watching and facilitating this discovery.

Cursing or Blessing Our Experience

If we know that something wonderful is going on, despite the way our personal beliefs make us feel, then we are able to make, in and through difficult experiences, blessed discoveries. I was up a great deal in the night with our second son, and at times it seemed like an ordeal that would never end. But one night, as I was walking the floor with the baby in my arms, I thought of how Zen students make themselves sit in terribly uncomfortable positions for long periods of time as an important aspect of their zazen, or meditation. I thought, "Well, this is my zazen. Instead of complaining to myself about it, let me use the time to meditate."

To complain, even silently, about our difficulties is to curse ourselves and our experience. Complaining fills consciousness with darkness, insisting on the negative as the reality of oneself and one's life. Since consciousness is our avenue to the Divine, letting complaining thoughts run unchecked amounts to keeping the door closed to the very Goodness that we are complaining we lack. No experience is, itself, the problem. When I stopped hating my nighttime vigils and was willing to use them as a time for constructive mental work, they became a blessing. One of my clearest realizations of divine Love came from such a night.

Erik was fussing and fussing and I couldn't seem to find out what was wrong. Nothing I did helped. As I sat by the crib, trying to figure out what was bothering him, I remembered a sentence I had read. It said something like, "The belief of a baby in pain reveals a lack of understanding of the truth that God is Love." I suddenly felt overwhelmed by ignorance and said out loud, "Oh, Eriky, we just don't know enough about Love." Eventually he went back to sleep, and I thought no more about it.

The next morning, having put the boys down for their

naps, I felt a strong urge to get out into the backyard for my meditation time. The moment I stepped out, I felt surrounded by Love. Everywhere I looked, the green and blooming garden seemed to speak of Love. The thought kept repeating: "You've got to be blind not to see this." I noticed in passing that the sense was not of something "out there" having changed, but of some inner veil having dropped, momentarily, revealing what is always the truth of Life. I knew that I would be "blind" again, and indeed, I was. But that one moment's glorious seeing has blessed my life from then on and encouraged my quest for the unveiled clarity of Loveliness.

The crisis of new motherhood — who is mother (and who is child) here? — is resolved by the discovery that *Life is all the motherness and childness there is or can be. I am not a little human mother trying to cope with an even littler human child, but my baby and I are "places" where those divine attributes of the one Life are expressing themselves.* My personal identity sense is expanded and refined by the increasing realization of spiritual identity, observable everywhere. Wherever we look, and particularly in nature, we can see that Life consists of mother/child qualities. Life is expressive, creative, supportive, nurturing, harmonious. It is everlastingly fresh, vital, pure, spontaneous.

The Second Baby

The mother's major identity shift takes place with the first baby, and we all know that motherhood with subsequent babies seems much easier, even if they are more difficult babies. There is a potential pitfall, however, in expecting our second baby to be like the first. Two children are likely to be opposites in many ways. When the first has been a relatively easy baby, the second may well be noisier and therefore more demanding. This doesn't mean that anything is wrong with the baby, and we need to beware of feeling negative or critical toward the second child just because he or she is not like the first. We are in for wonderful surprises if we can enjoy seeing the differences between our kids.

Seven months into motherhood, I found myself pregnant again. It seemed another crisis, yet I knew I would end up being glad. We wanted two children, and I would have found it hard to make a conscious decision to have another one. So I stopped crying and started thinking about a daughter. My Dutch husband ascertained, with a ring swinging on a cord, that the baby would be a girl — a Dutch superstition as far as I was concerned. We spent months deciding on the perfect girl's name, pausing only momentarily at the last moment to choose one for a boy. We pictured our daughter with golden curls, like her older brother.

What emerged, bellowing and broad-shouldered, was another boy, and one with straight, brown hair, at that. I giggled my way through the whole first day of post-Caesarean misery. What a joke on us! How delightful! Against the odds and despite our parental fantasies, this little guy presented himself in our midst. It was as if he were saying, "You may discover me but you cannot define me. I'm an original." The birth announcement his father had written seemed all the more appropriate:

> On the wings of the wind
> Of this greenhouse in space, earth,
> Comes drifting along
> *Een kind* . . . [Dutch for "a child"]
> Like a petal from the flower, man.
> A little boy,
> Our son and brother, Erik Jan,
>   for blooming.

And it's not only our babies who are here for blooming. We mothers bloom right along with them.

❧

MOTHER'S RESOURCE GUIDE for Chapter 2

Ideas To Ponder

And God said, Let us make man in our image, after our likeness. . . . So God created man in his own image. . . . And God saw everything that he had made, and, behold, it was very good. (Gen. 1:26–27, 31)

Know ye that the Lord, he is God: it is he that hath made us and not we ourselves; we are his people, and the sheep of his pasture. (Ps. 100:3)

There is only one Creator; whatever really exists is God's creation. We are not creators of children: we and our children are the creations of the one Mind. What does the Mind that is Spirit create? It creates spiritual ideas, such as beauty, harmony, vitality, love, joy, peace — the qualities of Being. These are the qualities that are the truth of us and our kids. We are made of Spirit's marvelous "stuff." This quality creation of God is all "very good."

Keeping this in mind, you can't go wrong as a mother. It is the mental atmosphere in the home that nurtures the child, not this or that specific practice of the parents. Don't think you can "blow it" by not scheduling right or by not responding correctly to the baby. And don't worry about "spoiling" the baby. Enjoy the baby and every day will bring you further evidence of his or her quality identity.

Every time a worry comes to mind, kick it "upstairs." This is God's show on both sides of the crib. Remember that God gives his angels charge over you and the baby, to keep you both in all your ways. The Universe is not asking of you nearly as much as you ask of yourself. The Universe asks only that you see what it is so dynamically being and doing.

Bedtime Ritual

Start right away developing a bedtime ritual that involves Good-seeing by talking to the baby about the nice things of the day. Then, when the baby begins to be able to join in, the pattern is already set. The importance of going to bed with a consciousness of goodness, rather than worries and stress, cannot be overestimated, for you and for the baby.

Rock and sing to the baby. There is a wonderful wholeness and oneness in such a moment of human intimacy, which is, at the same time, the nurturing and blessing of consciousness. For example, a spiritual truth, such as the one found in Jeremiah 23:24 — " 'Do not I fill heaven and earth,' saith the Lord" — becomes song/play for you and your baby as you sing a spiritual:

> He's got the whole world in His hands;
> He's got the big, wide world in His hands;
> He's got the whole world in His hands;
> He's got the whole world in His hands.
>
> He's got the itty bitty baby in His hands;
> He's got the little tiny baby in His hands;
> He's got the teeny weeny baby in His hands;
> He's got the whole world in His hands.

(This is a great spiritual to sing, because you can make up your own verses to fit the situation.)

> He's got the happy, loving momma in His hands;
> He's got the tired, stressed-out momma in His hands;
> He's got the momma and the poppa and the baby, too;
> He's got the whole world in His hands.

Infant Problems/Mother's Needs

Feeding, colic, crying, and fevers are common infant problems. Fear gives rise to physical symptoms and is then heightened by them. Therefore, dealing with her own anxiety is a mother's preeminent task. The Bible is full of the admonition: "Be not afraid!" so it must be possible to overcome fear.

When you have done whatever physically needs to be done for the baby, it is often useful to sit by the crib or, if necessary, hold the baby, and read something reassuring out loud. Read from the Bible or from any other spiritual literature that is meaningful to you. It is not necessary that the child understand what you read. Your presence and the sound of your voice are soothing and comforting. In our family, Jan often took night duty, because it was easier for him to do without sleep than for me. He would often read the Psalms. Psalm 91 is the great psalm of protection, and it is a good one to become familiar with and even to memorize.

There are also many tapes of hymns and readings that children like to listen to. A baby may find soft music or voices soothing, even before words are understood. The Christian Science Publishing Society puts out tapes for children. These may be purchased at any Christian Science Reading Room. As the kids get older, they can handle their own nighttime illnesses or restlessness by putting a tape in a Walkman and listening as they lie in bed. Our young adult sons still like to do this, and so do I. I'm not one for getting out of bed in the middle of the night to study, so a tape is just the thing. I have particularly profited from making tapes of my sessions with my spiritual guide and replaying these.

Meditations

> Be still, and know that I am God. (Ps. 46:10)

The following poem has been a pillar of my meditation for years:

BE STILL AND KNOW...
by Alan Aylwin

In the still and limpid pool of Godlike knowing, I bathed,
And cleansed of turbulence and fear,
  I stepped forth healed.

The healing came when, deep in rapt communion,
I saw that God in uninvaded stillness dwells.
  No self-willed drive exists in Him,
    no jarring, headlong rush...
Only the boundless, healing quiet of reality.

O restless one, dwell only in this tranquil moment!
  Immerse yourself in holy peace,
    sink deep in it.
See unlabored Being holding you and all,
within the warmth and rest of Its embrace.
  You, too, will come forth healed.[5]

Recommended Reading

Fraiberg, Selma, Ph.D. *The Magic Years*. New York: Charles Scribner's Sons, 1959. This is the best book I know of to provide an understanding of how the child thinks, from birth to six years of age. Humorous and compassionate.

Chapter 3

AGES ONE–FOUR

The Crisis of Trust / The Marvels of Understanding and Readiness

WHO'S IN CHARGE HERE?

I was six months pregnant and wheeling my thirteen-month-old son in his stroller when the young man stopped me.

"Pardon me," he said, "but I can't help noticing you. You are very courageous to have another baby again, so soon after the first." (I decided it wasn't necessary to confess that the "courage" was really an IUD failure, so I let the label stand.)

"We have a three-year-old and a new baby," he continued. "It's funny: when we had our first baby, we thought having a newborn was difficult. And it was! It practically ruined our marriage. But now, the newborn seems so easy, compared to the three-year-old!"

When our darling little babies become mobile and verbal, we begin the second stage of motherhood. I thought, at first, to call it "the crisis of will," because that's the way it often appears to the mother. Our "growth machines" seem to turn into "will machines" that operate just to defy and exasperate their parents. But that's only what seems to be, from the standpoint of that troublesome little ego sense of ours. It is really a crisis of trust. The need is for a foundation of trust beyond the interpersonal realm, so that it doesn't become an issue of interpersonal power. The personal answer to the question "Who's in charge?" is, "It's either me or him . . . and it had better be me!" Seen this way, the mother's need to find Life's trustworthiness is lost in the dynamics of trying to make the child obey her.

The Need To Get Beyond a Personal-Power Mindset

The crisis of trust involving toddlers is of great significance for two reasons. First of all, children between the ages of one and four are, of all age groups, the most likely to get a "bum rap." They are the least understood and therefore the most subject to unjust treatment. The fact that they cannot be trusted to make humanly mature decisions does not mean that they are either bad or disobedient, yet they are frequently treated as both. Secondly, the toddler crisis preshadows the teen crisis. If we don't get the personal power issue straight at this point, we will have hell to pay ten years down the line.

Perhaps the problem can best be illustrated by describing a scene that took place recently in a local post office. I was in line behind a mother with a little boy of about three. The mother insisted that the boy stand motionless at her side. The boy had other ideas. There was a window sill, two paces away, which was just his height and upon which he wanted very much to sit. But mother said, "No." She became increasingly frustrated, as her control attempts made the child more and more agitated. "You must learn to obey me absolutely," she insisted through clenched teeth, as she pinched his arm, making him squirm and fuss. Eventually, when the mother's turn came and she was distracted from him for a moment, the boy went to his longed-for destination and sat quietly on the sill until his mother finished.

What was striking to an observer of this scene was the

degree of stress that the mother was experiencing in the most ordinary circumstances. The five-minute wait became a substantial ordeal for her, and the failure to resolve it satisfactorily points to many ordeals to come. For such a mother, the preschool years with her child may become a daily crisis that can only get worse as the child gets older. The problem seems to be between her and the child, but that is precisely the mistaken belief that must be unmasked and healed, if the problem is ever to be resolved. She is trying to be a responsible mother, but she misperceives her responsibility as one big person needing to have personal power over one small person. She thinks a mother's job is to "make the kids behave." The very premise implies force and force creates resistance, and the force-and-resistance game is one that our children always win. But, as we have seen, what appear to be parent/child crises point us toward higher views of Life. Higher understanding is of absolute value in itself, and needs to be sought for itself, but it incidentally also yields better ways of coming at the issues that plague us.

We will never be able to get the crisis of trust resolved as long as our viewpoint is limited to a him-or-me power struggle. Obviously, very small children need curbs on their behavior. But the options are not limited to letting them run wild or else forcing them into submission. *We are concerned, as mothers, to be mentally present to the unfolding truth of things. Therefore we look at issues in order to understand rather than to control or punish.* When we understand our toddler's inner agenda, then we will see the most important truth about the behavior of young children: it is largely motivated by the demands of their developmental stage and not, as parents often think, by a conscious desire to defy parental authority.

The Toddler's Inner Agenda

Toddlers are experiencing the emergence of the sense of a separate self, and it is experienced as both a threat and a promise. The need to feel attached to the mother is still overriding, yet the developing capacities to walk, run, touch, and taste drive them to their expression and exploration. The toddler is not a "will machine" but an "expression/discovery machine." Young children are on the move, driven to actualize their new-found motor skills and increasing self-awareness in every possible way. This often gives the impression that they are "loose cannons," and anxious mothers may become preoccupied with tying the cannons down.

With a little ingenuity, toddlers can be kept safe without incessant friction. What becomes problematic is the belief that the young child thinks about things like an adult. When parents believe this, they invest too much in verbal control attempts and lose sight of the understanding work that needs to be done in their own thinking. Assuming that their little ones have the capacity to hear and obey their commands, parents perceive their failure to obey as disobedience, when it is, in fact, their obedience to the inner drive that it is their life task to obey at that moment. All that is going on in them, physiologically and mentally, is urging expression, the exploration of both their physical capacities and of the separate-self sense. This mostly overrides parental verbalization. I was endlessly grateful, during these early years with my own children, for a single sentence I had read in a book: "*Consistent obedience is impossible before the age of three.*" Quite apart from the fact that personal obedience is a distorted and troublesome concept, young children are not even capable of it until at least some time in their fourth year.

New Issues for Mothers

When infants turn into toddlers and begin to careen around the world in a way that may imperil both themselves and others, a mother's sense of responsibility mushrooms. Not only do we feel responsible for the child's welfare, but for that of others as well. In addition, we begin to feel vulnerable to other people's judgments about how well we are doing our job. We evaluate ourselves through the eyes of onlookers, and our children's behavior takes on the character of a report card on our mothering. This pressure from assumed judgments is a big factor in destroying a mother's poise and leading to behavior she later hates herself for.

Isolation is another factor in triggering a mother's frustration. I used to notice that without the mitigating presence of other adults I could get into a remarkably negative mindset with my two preschoolers. The high standard of living that places each mother in a detached single home sometimes seemed to me more like being stuck behind prison walls. I would think longingly of primitive societies, with a circle of huts and all the mothers and children working and playing together in the middle. Isolation heightens a mother's burdened sense of personal responsibility and can give rise to spasms of frustration and rage unthinkable at other times. It is good to notice this, but it is not good to condemn oneself for it. Self-condemnation turns instantly into toddler-condemnation, and a vicious cycle begins. We are not bad and they are not bad. We are, at such moments, blinded by some human belief that makes us all feel bad, and the belief that life is a matter of control of ourselves and/or others is often the culprit.

The correlation between self-abuse and child abuse is worth noting. In an abusive family, one child is usually the target, and that child is invariably the one most like the abusive parent. It is what we cannot tolerate in ourselves that we are most likely to attack in our children.

I noticed that I had the hardest time letting Tommy be himself, because he was most like me. He was like a mirror, and when I didn't like what I saw in the mirror, I experienced a compulsive urge to make it change. At times I felt like I needed to tape my mouth shut so that the stream of corrective injunctions couldn't run on. I learned increasingly to deal with my feelings as my own issue. Seeing myself as Love's expression and not a coping person, I experienced less and less self-demand and self-criticism. I became more able to let Tommy be, because I could let myself be.

The key to dominion over negative feelings is to keep and solve the issue in your own consciousness. Do not let it project onto others, because then you have two problems: your feelings and the pain and frustration that your projection has evoked in the other.

A Cultural Belief That Plagues Us

The real issue is never between the mother and the careening toddler, nor between the mother and the personal opinions of onlookers. The real issue lies in her understanding of Life. I notice a widespread and unexamined belief at large among parents in our society that goes as follows: "Children are, by nature, inclined to mischief and disobedience and must be made to be good, or they will be bad." Nothing could be further from the truth. There is no such thing as bad Life, and innocence and purity are essential childness qualities. The troubles that many parents have with their children are nothing but the results of that tragic misconception. *Starting from the premise that children must be forced to be good insures that their innate goodness will never be seen or respected, and the "bad child" of the parents' fantasy becomes a self-fulfilling prophecy.* Very often parents are unwittingly reflecting their own parents' view of them as bad, a verdict that has become a self-judgment, plaguing them throughout their lives.

The Seeing Principles

The shift from believing that motherhood is management to understanding our mother-task as seeing things from a truthful viewpoint gives us a precious key to our heart's dearest desire: to be a good mother. Thomas Hora states the principle of seeing: "As thou seest, so thou beest." Translated into practical form for mothers, the principle may be formulated in either negative or positive forms.

In its negative form, it becomes the Frankenstein Principle: *Paying attention to what you don't like in your kids' behavior creates monsters on both sides of the seeing.* The child's behavior tends to conform to your negative expectations, and your consciousness is filled with such ugly thought-forms as criticism, blame, frustration, and resentment.

Going back to the mother and boy in the post office, we can see the self-fulfilling prophecy at work before our eyes. The boy is grabbed, talked to in an angry voice, pinched, his arm twisted in a deliberately pain-inflicting way. He is told that absolute obedience to his mother is required. But why? What he wants is something perfectly reasonable, and the absolute personal obedience is not perfectly reasonable. He just wants to sit on a window sill that has his name on it.

But the poor mother is being pinched by the fear that her son is making her look bad in the eyes of other people. She feels abused at having to stand in line, trying to write a check with a squirming three-year-old to control, and having to do all this with strangers looking on only makes it worse. The more she tries to prove her control of the situation, the more the boy disproves it. We see monster child and monster mother developing right in front of us.

Nowhere within the mother's terms of understanding is there a foundation for trust. She cannot trust her son; she tries to trust her ability to control him and fails. The crisis of trust, unresolved, yields the hell of a personal power struggle in which everybody loses and everybody feels bad.

In its positive form, the law of seeing becomes the Fairy Godmother Principle: *Spiritual seeing transforms human identity into spiritual identity in both the seer and the seen.* To see your child's quality identity is to be transformed into your own quality identity — the ultimately good Mother. Blessing the child by seeing him or her as a place where Life is manifesting Its qualities, you become, likewise, a place where the divine Life is expressing Itself.

What is a fairy godmother? She is a magical presence who can, with the wave of a wand, transform frogs into princes and scullery maids into princesses. Why? Usually because that was the truth of their identity before an evil spell was cast upon them. A fairy godmother removes spells to reveal the royal presence that was hidden within. Spiritual seeing is a mental rather than a physical wand, but it likewise removes the spells of personal sense that curse us and our children with evil labels.

These two principles of seeing apply not only to mother/child issues but to every aspect of our lives. The urgency of our concerns as mothers, however, gives us extra incentive to pay attention to what viewpoint we are accepting as our thinking. When I would notice the grouchiness and sense of burden that plagued my early mothering years, I would utilize the question introduced in chapter 2 and ask myself, "What belief about myself is feeling this way?" This enabled me to unmask the false drama of too-much-demand/too-little-supply that belonged to my human way of thinking.

Right away it would be clear that my little boys were not abusing me, so the bad feelings tended to stay on my side and not be projected onto them. Then I would remind myself that God wasn't seeing an abused woman; God was seeing a house full of Love. Even though the bad feelings didn't just evaporate, they never became dominant in my relations with the boys.

The belief that our role is to be managers puts us on the defensive, against our children, and this creates the crisis of trust. We know we cannot trust them, and we are afraid we cannot trust ourselves. This crisis can be resolved only by understanding. Trust cannot be forced. We cannot make ourselves trust something we do not understand. And it is very difficult for us to understand when we think our task is to be managers of behavior.

"Understanding" is defined as "the clear perception of the meaning of something." The first level of trust is to trust that something understandable is going on, even if we don't know yet what it is. That trust leads us to take the time to consider what is happening and gives us a beginning sense of dominion that helps us to be open to solving the problem through intelligence rather than force.

Inviting Inspiration

Parents are always tripped up when they try to manage or control a situation before they have taken time to understand what is going on. As a family counselor, I notice that parents always come in wanting to know, "What shall we do?" I answer, "How can we know what to do until we understand what is going on?" Parents feel an unreasonable demand upon them to do something to fix things before they have the understanding that would yield a solution. They then tend to pass on the unreasonable demands to their children, who feel neither trusted nor understood.

Mothers, who must take care of a multitude of family business details with young children in tow, are particularly hampered by the belief that they can't take time to understand or intelligently deal with a problem. Recently I waited in a shop along with a mother and her two preschoolers. The constant interaction between the children reminded me of how difficult it seems when we try to divide our attention between the business that must be conducted and squabbling kids. A dispute arose, which the mother heightened by a shouting/punishing reaction that was just the expression of her frustration and embarrassment. But happily, a moment later the mother, clearly regretting her outburst, took time to really listen to the children, and she then made an intelligent suggestion that settled the conflict. The incident reminded me how sheer survival concerns had led me, like this mother, to notice that taking a moment to give full attention to the boys' issues could lead to a quick, simple resolution, which then left me free to conduct the business at hand.

A fear of not knowing what to do if we do pay attention to our kids may underlie our reluctance to do so. But the reverse is true: the act of being mentally present to the situation invites inspired ideas. We do not personally have to know what to do about our kids or anybody else. Our appeal is to universal Intelligence or Mind, rather than to our own or our children's seeming little minds. To make the appeal we need only be silent for a moment in the acknowledgment of a higher Intelligence. This immediately lifts our consciousness into the light of universal Mind, and "in thy light do we see light" (Ps. 36:9). It is God's guidance, in the form of inspired understanding, that we come to trust, not ourselves as persons nor our children as persons.

Life does not demand blind action, even though people

sometimes do. The real need is always to see something. It makes an enormous difference in our thinking about issues with preschool children if our focus of attention is on understanding something ourselves rather than on controlling their behavior. And the marvel is that being learners rather than managers is all that is required of us. The understanding "does" itself, for us, if we are open to it, and the understanding does the controlling.

I still gratefully remember a brief experience I had with our younger boy when he was two. Jan and I and the boys were coming in late to a meeting in which people were sitting in meditative silence. Wanting our entrance to be as unnoticed as possible, I scooped Erik up in my arms as we wiggled our way past people to find a seat. To my amazement — and acute embarrassment — the moment I picked him up, he began to scream. As I sat with this screeching fellow on my lap, I first tried to hush him, which, of course, only made him scream harder. I then thought of getting up and taking him out, but suddenly I was stuck with understanding. "You wanted to walk in, didn't you?" I whispered to him. He stopped crying immediately and nodded. I let him slip off my lap. He toddled the few paces to the door, turned around, toddled back, and sat contentedly and silently on my lap for the rest of the time. After the meeting, a woman expressed to me her great appreciation and enjoyment of that vignette.

This was a very inspiring experience for me, for it was not anything I could have anticipated or done. At the very moment when my personhood was all wrapped up in trying to manage an embarrassing situation, divine Love and Intelligence saw and responded to the issue. Erik's concern was perfectly legitimate, to his sense of things. He was a big boy now. He could walk on his own. It was my own lack of trust that created the crisis, as I assumed that he would cause a disturbance if I left him on his own. Yet Love rescued us both. And even the concern about what other people would think was taken care of.

In this instance, once I understood Erik's issue, I was able to let him do what he wanted. Often this is not the case with toddlers. Yet when clarity comes, it always includes inspired solutions. Toddlers have extremely short attention spans and can therefore be quickly distracted from their snits. Had we been sitting too far from the door to let Erik go back and walk in, a promise to let him walk out would probably have sufficed. If not, some other idea would have surfaced.

The wonderful thing about understanding is that it yields a broad range of behavior. It is much more practical than specific advice about what action to take. We may think we would like to be told what to do, but I have often found that I was unable to do what was recommended by others. The more we are clear about what's going on, the freer we are to behave in any way that fits the situation. For example, though scooping Erik up for our entrance didn't work in this instance, it is often the action to take with a toddler in other circumstances. When we need to go and our toddlers are dawdling, it is easiest simply to pick them up, despite their protests. They will forget their frustration and stop screaming the moment something else is offered for them to pay attention to. I see parents hollering at toddlers to come, becoming frustrated at their obliviousness to the commands, and then slapping or spanking them for their supposed disobedience, when a simple "toddler-scoop" would take care of the situation.

Seeing Quality Identity Facilitates Understanding

The behavior of children at this age can seem completely perplexing and exasperating. Mothers who see themselves as personally in charge can feel particularly confused about setting limits. If we think about things from a personal stand-point, we will always end up either indulging or frustrating our children, or ourselves. But if we see that we and our kids are "places" where Life is blooming, in the form of its own qualities and according to its own lawfulness of good, we have an entirely different experience. Then we marvel again and again to see how clearly the intelligence and harmony of Being can be seen, despite the belief in little and big persons and personal minds. We discover from this that what is going on with our kids always makes sense, if we just take the time to notice it. There is a direct correlation between trust-ing that the truth of our kids is spiritual qualities and making sense of their human agendas and needs.

A young father, whom we'll call Sam, presented the following problem:

> I work nights and my wife works days, so I am home in our small apartment with our two children much of the time. I have a barrier around our TV so that the kids can't get to it to fiddle with the knobs, which they love to do. But Elly, who is eighteen months old, just won't stay away.
>
> I sit there and watch her head straight for the TV. I say, "No!" She keeps right on. I shout at her, "No, Elly, do not touch! That's no!" She pays no attention. I get up and pick her up and give her a swat and say, "No!" She cries and sits still for a few moments and then she's at it again. She looks right at me as she heads straight for the forbidden object. I'm beginning to think that "no" means something different to her than to me!

Sam is to be congratulated for calling into question the failure of his method. He sees that there is something for him to understand. And he's right that "no" doesn't mean to the toddler what it means to the parents. As we have already discussed, children of this age cannot reason in adult obedience terms. But because his thinking is very much governed by personal power and obedience beliefs, he could not notice that, as I put it to him: "You are emphasizing what's 'no.' But what's 'yes'?" The toddler's agenda is exploration. She is confined to a small apartment where all attention is focused on a big box in the middle with an intriguing fence around it. She is drawn to it like a magnet, and the fact that Dad keeps being weird and shouting and spanking doesn't in the least impact on her inner exploration agenda.

If Dad wants to shift the focus of that agenda — and this is what is needed — he will need to come up with a "yes," that is, something interesting to be explored. Even a small apartment contains lots of possibilities for toddler fun. Many mothers discover early on that a couple of pots and pans and a wooden spoon or two are more interesting to children this age than most of the too-fancy, expensive toys that may look intriguing to adults. *If our heads are not cluttered by the bad-child and personal power beliefs, then we may be able to understand what is needed, and the understanding itself comes up with the ideas that easily meet the need.* It is not something we can or need to do personally, and that is the marvel of it.

Understanding and Love Are One

Understanding and love are inseparable. We know that from our own experience. We know that if someone says, "I love you" but shows that they do not understand us, we do not feel loved. Conversely, feeling understood by someone, we feel loved, though that person might never say so. But understanding is not really an interpersonal thing. We are not dependent upon another person for it. It is an event in consciousness. It is always available if we are interested in it. In fact, it is the truth of us and our children as well. This is illustrated by the fact that *children themselves want to understand, love to understand, if we will just take the time to be understandable.* Even before toddlers can speak they can understand a great deal of what we are saying. The understanding demonstrated by our boys when they were toddlers was a constant source of amazement to my husband, who had been raised in a strict European home in which small children were given little credit for anything except being nuisances that had to be tightly controlled.

Preschoolers bring us back again and again to our own thinking as the place of dominion, because attempts to control them interpersonally bring on experiences of such frustration. Just getting things done with a couple of preschool children around may seem quite a feat. During those early years, I would often pile into the car with my two boys, off on several errands. The errands were simple: picking up the cleaning, taking something to be repaired, shopping for groceries. But each stop meant little persons getting out of the car, little persons getting into strollers, little persons fussing to get out of strollers or fussing to get into grocery carts... and then back into the car, and little persons dawdling, and wiggling when they were being strapped in. By the time we got back home, I would feel harassed to the hilt.

But one day, as I was impatiently waiting for them to disembark from such a trip, understanding struck again. The thought came: "They are not hassling me. I am hassling them, and myself, by mentally pushing them all the time." I could see that my stressed sense came from my unwillingness to respect their agenda, and my own as well. I was not only an errand-runner. I was, most importantly, a mother. And a mother's agenda is understanding and providing for quality living. The boys did not ask to go along running errands. That activity did not in any way meet their needs. So if it was necessary, I would have to broaden my view of the situation.

After that I would either try to do shopping and errands at a time when the children could be left with someone, or I would make our trips a joint venture, planning them to include the boys' needs and interests in some way. A stop at a donut shop, mid-trip; letting them pick one small treat in a grocery store to hold and keep track of until we went through the checkstand; noticing and pointing out bright colors or interesting displays — the possibilities are endless. I see many mothers doing this with their children as they grocery shop, and it is always a delight to observe. I enjoyed the daily round so much more when it was done in a context of making sure we all had a good time.

Looking Through the Eyes of Love

While in seminary, I babysat frequently for the four children of one of my professors. I learned much from the children's mother, Sydney, a very bright and artistic woman who was wholeheartedly invested in motherhood. My tight, do-things-right sense was continually illuminated and relieved by her easy presence. One winter day I prepared to take the two younger children out to play in the snow. I finished bundling the two-year-old boy into his snow suit, boots, mittens, hat, and scarf. As we stood back and surveyed the resultant heap of paraphernalia, with the cherub face peeking out, Sydney commented, "I find certain sizes and shapes very appealing."

Something about that remark made a deep impression on me. Its understated, non-personal affection and appreciation summed up the mentality with which she participated in, yet stayed above, the multitudinous tasks inundating a mother of four. The adorableness of that little figure, nearly immobilized by the protective winter clothing, was not taken for granted nor dismissed. The continual noticing of the special attributes of each age is a major source of pleasure for a mother. Sydney enjoyed motherhood because she was so present to it, so ready to find joy in the delightful details in the midst of the daily routine.

The Marvel of Readiness

Despite a mother's occasional points of feeling at loggerheads with an obstinate toddler, these years illustrate the order and harmony of Life in a particularly delightful way. It is what educators call "readiness," and to me it seemed miraculous. Readiness refers to the sense of an inner timetable, which we noticed in the first year. It suggests that when children are ready to move on to the next stage, be it physical, mental, emotional, or behavioral, they will do so. It says, in essence, that nothing needs to be forced. Just knowing that is an enormous liberation to parents.

I particularly remember noticing readiness in terms of floating. While vacationing at a mountain lake, I watched Tommy splashing along with his hands on the bottom, pushing and supporting himself. Back and forth he went until, suddenly, he was floating. He just "forgot" to put his hands down, and he was floating. And then, as is always the case, he couldn't get enough of it!

Having watched this process with Tommy, I was prepared for an issue that came up later with Erik. He was signed up for swimming lessons, but when we arrived the first morning he didn't want to get into the water. Feeling sure that I could trust the principle of readiness, I was able to respect his reticence, and we spent the first day sitting on the side watching. The next day he joined the class without hesitation. The swim staff recommended forcing fearful

kids into the water. Another mother let her boy be dragged screaming into the pool and dunked until he stopped crying. She looked at me with anguish in her eyes and said, "I just don't know what's right to do. They say this is the best way." But I could see that she hated what was happening and really wanted to stop it.

For the mother the issue is not so much what she decides is best in any given situation. There is no perfect human mother and no "only" way to handle swimming lessons or music lessons or any of the other things that come up. But it is important for a mother to have a basis of certainty that gives her direction and enables her to trust her own judgment. There is nothing more unbearable to a mother than being called upon to make decisions that affect her child's welfare and feeling unsure of what is best. The most trustworthy basis for decisions is the understanding of what Life is and how it works, rather than any particular human theory of the moment. *Readiness is the principle that reveals to us that no positive step needs to be forced. Parents cooperate with readiness by providing opportunities for their children to experience and express what they are ready for.* But we are delivered from the dilemma of wondering where and when we must force certain behaviors on a child.

We are mothers because the motherness qualities of Life are such a substantial part of the divine Nature that they assert themselves everywhere. Our interest is the richest possible experience of mothering. We not only want to suffer as little as possible; we want to be inspired and inspiring mothers, to feel that we make a valuable contribution. We will be continually disappointed if we think our contribution must be personal. This belief leads us to feel a constant sense of demand and fear of personal inadequacy. It also tends to make us look for personal recognition and appreciation from others for our good work.

The truth is that we feel most beneficial and fulfilled in those moments of understanding in which we feel in tune with a larger Intelligence and Good. Then we feel enveloped in a sense of blessedness that includes not only our own children but everyone and everything.

"With God All Things Are Possible"

All mothers regret deeply the inevitable moments of negativity between them and their children. Guilt is a constant in every mother's mentality. It is, therefore, a gift of grace to realize that we've never "blown it" so badly that Love/understanding cannot rescue us. I love the assurance Jesus gives to his disciples when they ask him, "Who then can be saved?" His reply is "The things which are impossible with men are possible with God" (Luke 18:27). The compassion of this fact was brought home to me in one of my worst-mothering moments by the youngest person in the room. The boys must have been about three and four, and Tommy, the four-year-old, was angry at me. He picked up the lid of the sugar bowl of a new set of stoneware and dangled it above the kitchen floor. He was a very dutiful child, and I couldn't believe he would deliberately drop something he knew was precious to me. But he did, and it shattered. I burst into tears and started wailing, "Oh, Tommy, how could you do that to me. How could you break my new china...." I was vaguely aware that something in me was carrying it too far, but I couldn't seem to stop. I wanted him to sob repentance...I wanted him to say, "I'm so sorry, Mommy." But he sat in numb silence, a single tear running down one cheek. Finally Erik came over to me and said, "Mommy, God doesn't want you to cry like that."

Immediately, the mesmerism of interpersonal manipulation was broken, and I felt deeply embarrassed. I sputtered for a moment, trying to justify the outburst to myself, but the balloon had been punctured and the sputtering died out. I thanked Erik for his lovely, truthful statement, cleaned up the broken china and went on with the chores. Later, I saw clearly that Tommy was shocked and confused by my reaction and reacted in the only way he could. The more I insisted on the response I wanted, the more immobilized and confused he became. When I saw that, I spoke to Tommy about how much I regretted my behavior and how glad I was that God had helped me out of it.

From this and similar incidents throughout the boys' preschool years, I learned a lesson of great value. I learned to stick with the issue and forget the hysterics. The hysterics always cloud the issue. They are based on a desire to manipulate the response of the other person, and they always boomerang. Even very small children can understand issues. When emotional reactions are added, children become distracted by fear and anger, and then we have another level of problem to deal with.

Seeing Through the Belief in Personal Obedience

The marvels of readiness and understanding show us that *we don't have to be personally obedient to anyone else. Nor do we have to insist that our children be personally obedient to us. Life is living itself in perfect obedience to its own nature.* Children cannot help obeying the forces of growth and development that drive them. Seeing this, we find ourselves manifesting the qualities of love and intelligence in ways we would never be able to on our own. It comes down to this: Life does motherness and childness a lot better than we or our kids could ever do on the basis of personal identity.

"Mommy, God doesn't want you to cry like that." Mother, Life doesn't want you to cry at all. It is the human, limited sense of things, calling itself our identity, that cries and hollers and suffers. Motherhood is a wonderful school in which to learn the lessons that graduate us from such miseries. Whose blindness wouldn't be enlightened by the sweet face of a three-year-old pleading God's Love? In no other context of human life do the lessons come in lovelier, more positive ways. Our love for our children encourages, rather than forces, our quest for greater understanding of the divine, universal lovingness of Life. The gifts of each stage of motherhood supply our readiness for the next. "O [wo]man, greatly beloved, fear not: peace be unto thee, be strong, yea, be strong" (Dan. 10:19).

❧

MOTHER'S RESOURCE GUIDE for Chapter 3

And the Lord shall guide you continually,
And satisfy your desire with good things,
And make your bones strong.
And you shall be like a watered garden,
Like a spring of water, whose waters fail not.
(Isa. 58:11, RSV)

The Wonder Years

At no other age are children as ready, willing, and able to look at things with wonder as they are in their toddler and preschool years. Our own seeing becomes new again as we see every detail of the daily round through their fresh vision. The daily activities become a kind of wonder-collecting, because so many small details are new and interesting to the young child's expanding awareness. Consciously and verbally participating with them in the discovery process greatly enhances a routine that, to an adult, is old hat and devoid of interest. Such things as traffic lights and supermarket scanners can be rediscovered as wondrous evidences of order and intelligence.

> Every material belief hints the existence of spiritual reality; and if mortals are instructed in spiritual things, it will be seen that material belief, in all its manifestations, reversed, will be found the type and representative of verities priceless, eternal and just at hand.[6]

I love the phrase "verities priceless, eternal and just at hand." Our children provide us with so many opportunities to notice that the ultimate, priceless goods of Life are "just at hand." When we are even a little bit "instructed in spiritual things" we become able to see through material belief to these grand truths of Life.

Tommy's Race

At the end of the summer just before he went to kindergarten, Tommy entered a race. The City Parks' Department was holding an all-city Play Day for children. Activities were structured for different age groups. A hundred-yard dash was offered for five-year-olds, and Tommy wanted to compete. He was a pretty speedy little fellow among his neighborhood playmates, so we thought he might even have a chance of winning.

The morning of the race, with Erik in tow, I took him over to the stadium where the race was to be held. We got there a few minutes before starting time, and I was shocked to see that other parents were taking the race very seriously. Most children were with their fathers, who were coaching them and timing them on practice runs. I only had time to point out the start and finish lines to Tommy before the race began. The children lined up, the referee shouted, "On your marks! Get set," and then fired a starting gun.

Tommy was startled by the gunshot, which he had not

expected, and paused an instant to be sure he was supposed to run. By that time, the other kids were well down the field. Tommy then ran as hard as he could until just before the finish line, at which point he slowed down and stopped, precisely on the line.

He look up at me, his face beaming. "Did I win, Mom?" he asked. Some of the other parents, standing nearby, laughed, and I laughed too and said, "No, honey, you didn't win."

I felt very embarrassed. He was so out of it, so oblivious to the fact that he came in last and looked pretty silly stopping right on the finish line. My mind was a muddle of personal feelings, and I was casting about, trying to think of what to say to him. But before I could get another word out, he started to chatter excitedly.

"I'm going to tell Daddy that I ran a real race, on a real track, and there was a starting gun and everything." His face was aglow. He turned to his brother. "Did you see me, Erik. Did you see me run the hundred-yard dash? I never ran in a real race before. This was a real race. They had starting blocks and everything!"

On and on he chattered, his eyes bright, a big smile on his face. Tears suddenly stung my eyes. The innocence of his response stunned me. The discrepancy between his sweet enthusiasm and my self-centered parental concerns with how he and I looked in other people's eyes made me ashamed. He had run a race and loved it. He loved the running, the participation, the activity. He was not yet corrupted by the need to win or to look impressive in other people's eyes. I felt myself to be the unworthy recipient of a very great gift.

For months after that, every time we drove by that stadium, Tommy would joyfully announce: "That's where I ran my race!" And every time he said it, the purity of his seeing surprised and moved me afresh.

I am the God who is near, says the Lord God, and not a God afar off. (Jer. 23:23, Lamsa tr.)

Testimony

One of my favorite types of spiritual reading has always been testimonies by individuals who have experienced healings and moments of enlightened seeing. The Christian Science periodicals offer a regular diet of healing testimonies. *The Three Pillars of Zen* and *Zen, Dawn in the West*, books by Phillip Kapleau, contain testimonies of enlightenment through the practice of Zen meditation. A recent book, *The Relevance of Bliss* by Nona Coxhead, explores the spontaneous mystical seeing events of many individuals. This testimony comes from a book long out of print called *Watchers on the Hill* by Raynor Johnson.

"NOT MY WILL…"

On one occasion I felt particularly helpless. It was not a dramatic situation by the usual standards. My two sons, aged ten and eight, were quarrelling in the adjacent room. It was a typically childish argument over a trifle, but I felt part of me rising up in annoyance and impatience. I was tired after a long day. My three-year-old daughter was sitting at the table repeatedly refusing to eat her dinner. My husband, perhaps with some justification not apparent to me at the time, gruffly demanded his customary but hitherto overlooked cup of tea.

The boys began to endanger themselves with their fighting. In that instant, I knew that the irritability of the lower half of my personality would explode into a disproportionately angry outburst. Even as I walked toward the boys with my hands raised ready to thrust them apart roughly, I cried out to my God in my heart. (I cannot describe my earnestness simply as prayer — it was very much a cry to God. It was actually wordless, a rapid thinking experience without the use of words — but I cannot convey that to paper.) As nearly as I can describe it my approach to God was, "Lord, I love them. I do not want to hurt them. Left to myself I am helpless. Help me, my God! I freely submit my will, my mind, everything that is in me — for their sakes!" As I arrived at the spot where the boys stood, I found that it was not I who acted at all. I felt that some power other than myself controlled me, but it was a power of love which could be trusted. My hands were gentle as I separated the combatants — I could feel the love flowing out toward them — and they instantly clung one to each side of me, both smiling lovingly and happily up at me. In their eyes was a simple trust that I have never seen in them before or since. If I attempted to explain what happened, I could only suggest that the tremendous love surging out from me flowed unhindered into their simple and uncluttered child-minds.

I then turned to the baby and spoke to her. It was as if it were not I who determined what words were to be spoken. I do not even remember what they were. I do know, however, that my voice was gentle, and that the little one picked up her spoon and began to eat contentedly. I turned to my husband and found him quietly preparing the tea.

For the brief space of time here outlined, I was an entirely different personality. There was no "self" demanding attention. . . . The most vivid impression was that my will had disappeared. And yet I was free.

This story illustrates the spontaneous shifting of consciousness from the dreary level of personal egos, each with its own demands and gripes, to the level of God's seeing, where Love and intelligence govern the whole scene. Notice how, when the mother's "self" and "will" dissolved, those mental states of her husband and children dissolved as well. This is a principle of consciousness: self begets and reinforces self, whereas selflessness begets selflessness. Note, too, that what was there, when personal ego dissolved, was "a power of love which could be trusted."

Though we may not have such dramatic experiences, reports like this confirm to us that we "live and move and have our being" in Something far bigger and better than we are usually aware of. This evidence enables us to acknowledge this divine Presence even when we cannot see or feel it humanly. The mother in the story didn't see it at the beginning either. But so absolute was her desire to let God be present instead of her personality that the very appeal to God, wordless as it was, brought about the shift in seeing. Our extremity *is* God's opportunity simply because the personal ego sense is more ready to get out of the way when its pretenses to power and good are stripped away.

O taste and see that the Lord is good: blessed is the man that trusteth in him. (Ps. 34:8)

Recommended Reading

Berends, Polly. *Gently Lead: Or How to Teach Your Children about God While Finding Out for Yourself*. New York: HarperCollins, 1991. This is a wonderful compendium of parent/child dialogues about God and the big issues of Life, with Polly Berends's wise commentary interspersed.

Chapter 4

AGES FIVE–TWELVE
The Crisis of Performance /
The Marvel of Spiritual Dominion

WHAT'S GOING TO HAPPEN TO HIM/ME OUT THERE?

I remember vividly the first day of our first son's public schooling. His kindergarten teacher was known to be both excellent and tough, a woman of competence and conviction. As we stood in line she greeted the children one by one by kneeling down to address them at their level. The little boy in front of us was named Thomas, as was our son. The teacher asked him what he liked to be called, and he said, "Tommy." When she got to us, she said that our Tommy would have to choose another form of the name in order to avoid confusion. He chose "Tom."

I felt devastated. I wanted to fuss and protest. I wanted to say, "But Tommy is his name. 'Tom' is too old. You can't change his name just for classroom convenience." It seemed a violation of his identity.

It seems funny now to remember how upset I was that Tommy wouldn't be called that in his kindergarten class. It was never any problem to him, and it didn't change what I called him at home. I think it was so upsetting because it symbolized a mother's major crisis during the school years: the loss of direct control over the child's situation and welfare.

Most children have already had some experience in pre-school by the time they enter public school, so that first day is no longer the dramatic moment of the child's first venture outside the home. Even so, public school is an enormous expansion of the child's — and therefore the mother's — world, and it brings its share of crises. Even parents who choose private schools cannot avoid facing the challenges of this period. Children become, more and more, members of society: they join teams and organizations and groups. They come under the demands and influence of other adults and other children. We worry about these demands: "Are they right? Are they fair? Can our child meet them?" And we worry about the influences: "Can we make wise decisions about what is good and what is not good? Can we protect our children from harmful influences? Can our children discriminate between good and bad suggestions?"

Beware of the Blame Game

In addition to these concerns about our children and their performance and safety, we often feel that our own performance, as mothers, is being judged by others. We feel blamed by school officials if our children are having problems in the school setting. It is the nature of personal sense to react to a fear of being blamed by blaming others. Teachers are the first to become targets of parental blame, and parents and teachers tend to get locked in a very self-defeating blame game. Each side, expecting to be blamed by the other, enters every discussion of the child's situation in a defensive mindset.

Blame mentality is a major problem during these years. It is a devil, an evil thought form, that curses everyone whom it touches. Blame is an unavoidable aspect of the belief that our well-being depends upon personal performance. Blame is the personal ego's defense against discovering that Life is not, actually, personally manageable. Blaming says in effect, "This bad thing did not need to happen. It could have been avoided if I/he/she/they had just done it right." In this way the false beliefs that life is a matter of personal management and that persons are capable of that task are maintained.

The real problem is that both beliefs are mistaken. As we have been graced to notice during our children's early years, Life is not a personal project but a transpersonal unfoldment. The more we try to exert personal control over its details, the more we obscure from our awareness the order and benevolence of Being. If we let blame constitute the framework of our thinking, we find ourselves feeling always blameworthy, anxious, and defensive. Worse, we end up blaming our children, which only leads them to feel blameworthy, anxious, and defensive and teaches them to blame others as a way of trying to manage their own fears.

In this regard, I often think of a mother I counseled some years ago. She had a seven-year-old boy who was in constant trouble at home and at school. I talked with her several times and then asked to see the boy, since the problem was not clear to me. I saw mother and son together first and noticed that before the boy had moved a muscle, the mother was already anticipating trouble and trying to prevent it by correcting him. If he stirred in his seat, he was angrily told, "Sit still!" When I attempted to talk with him directly the mother interrupted, answering for him and describing him in negative ways.

I then spoke with the boy alone and found no evidence of severe pathology. He was friendly, communicative, and energetic. It seemed to me that he probably caused problems in the classroom simply because, since every natural impulse was labeled "bad" by his mother, he had not developed any sense of permissible forms of activity.

Talking with the mother alone, I shared my observations

and spoke about how important it was to give the boy positive feedback so that he could learn to think of himself as good. We spoke of ways to help him distinguish between troublesome and constructive behavior. She seemed to understand what I was saying. But when the boy came back in, and I told him I would not need to see him again because I thought he was just fine, the mother broke in to exclaim, "She doesn't want to see you again because you are so bad!"

I was stunned. Mothers love their children and want only the good for them. What belief could make a woman lie about what I had said, right in front of me, and harshly discredit her own son? To me, this mother's frantic accusation of her son revealed the depth of her anxiety about herself and her ability to meet the demands she felt put upon her. The school pressured her to "do something" about her son's behavior. But everything she did only seemed to make matters worse. Not being able to bear the sense of responsibility and inadequacy, she could find relief only by seeing her son as inherently bad. If he is bad, then his behavior is explainable and she is not to blame. If the mother cannot bear the sense of responsibility and inadequacy, how can the child be expected to bear it? Mother and son are not adversaries. They are both victims of the unrecognized cultural suggestion that we have to be gods, the creators and shapers of our lives.

The Punishment Quandary

The crisis of blame yields a secondary crisis for mothers, and that is punishment. If someone is to blame, that person needs to be punished. The blame belief — that someone *should* have done differently — presumes that that person *could* have done differently. If this is the case, that person must have consciously and freely chosen to do the wrong thing. This reasoning leads inevitably to the need for some sort of deterrent. One must make the wrong choice painful enough that the individual will not want to choose it again.

Punishment, however, has its own set of difficulties. It is hard to know when and how and how much to punish. It often does not seem to help. Punishment always induces resentment in children because there is a personal power element in punishment, which, as we learned with our toddlers, complicates and clouds the issues. Mothers may have particular difficulty with punishment, because they are so psychologically in tune with their children's feelings. Many is the home in which a mother, in desperation, declares, "Just wait until your father comes home!" But setting Dad up as the punisher is not desirable either. So what's a poor mother to do?

The following story is a kind of riddle that introduces an intriguing angle on the blame/punishment issue:

A little boy of eight was sent home from school with a note from the teacher stating that he had been unmanageable. He had been hitting little girls with his fist and had tripped his friend, with the disastrous result that the friend broke two front teeth.

The mother of the boy was, naturally, quite upset and her first impulse was to devise a punishment that would really "teach the boy a lesson." The thought occurred to her that the most severe punishment she could inflict on him would be to take away his dog.

She consulted her psychiatrist, who told her to make sure she understood the meaning of the child's behavior before she took punitive action. When, however, no understanding was forthcoming, she was led to consider the meaning of her idea that the most severe punishment would be to deprive the child of his dog, his cherished possession. This seemed to indicate a belief that the worst thing that could happen to a person was to be separated from his cherished possession.

The mother admitted that indeed she was inclined to love rather possessively, and whenever she thought herself in danger of losing any of her cherished possessions, she tended to become belligerent, angry and depressed. At this point, the question arose whether perhaps the little boy, too, was in danger of losing something which he considered a cherished possession.

The mother said, "I cannot think of anything. As a matter of fact, my son was very happy because his grandparents were planning to stay in our house while my husband and I would be on vacation... was the prospect of separation from us the problem? Of course, that must be the meaning of it! What should be done? Should we cancel our vacation and stay home?"

The psychiatrist replied, "If you cancel your vacation and stay home, you will confirm and gratify the child's possessive notion of love. If you go away, you will frustrate his possessive notion of love. In either case, you will reinforce his possessive notion of love. It seems that right now, staying home would be no solution, nor would leaving help. You cannot punish the child, nor can you condone what he has done. You cannot blame yourself, nor are you without responsibility."

"What, then, is the solution?" asked the mother.

"That's a good question," answered the doctor.[7]

By not supplying an immediate solution, the psychiatrist forces the mother — and us — to a level of thinking beyond what to do to "fix" our children. The story helps us see how naive the blame/punishment way of thinking is. It completely misses the point. *Children do not choose to misbehave. Behavior is the product of belief, and it is therefore the underlying belief, rather than the behavior, that needs to be addressed.* More-over, children are not the creators of the beliefs that operate as their thinking. At this age, they largely mirror their parents' beliefs. But parents are not the creators of "their" beliefs either. We must beware of simply shifting blame: "The child is misbehaving... therefore the parents must be thinking wrong."

The beliefs from which we all suffer are always some form of the universal, human misconception of Life in which we are on our own and separate from any larger, reliable Source. Consequently, we seem to be personally responsible for our well-being and that of our children. This misconception is troublesome in any and every form and variation, and the trouble therefore alerts us to the presence of the mistaken be-lief. There is always something to understand: a false belief to unmask and a truth to discover. *Blaming short-circuits the understanding process.* Employing the Fairy Godmother Prin-ciple and starting from the acknowledgment that positive, spiritual qualities are the truth of the child, we stay out of the blame trap, and the false beliefs that underlie the problem are more likely to surface and be seen.

In this enlightening riddle, the misconception of love as personal possession is exposed. The boy is not to blame for the mistaken idea nor is the mother. Its exposure is the ac-tivity of truth bringing it out into the open so that it may be replaced by the wondrous discovery of Love as a uni-versal principle, always and everywhere in operation. The boy's school problem may end up leading the mother to discoveries about Life that release and heal her as well as her son. The outcome of spiritual problem-solving often in-volves such liberating discoveries that the solution itself is felt to be secondary.

Discipline and Punishment Are Mutually Exclusive

Many mothers think that the terms "discipline" and "punishment" are the same, but they are not. The root of the word "discipline" is a Latin term meaning "learner." The Latin root for the word "punishment" is also the root of the word "pain." So the aim of discipline is learning, and the aim of punishment is to inflict pain. The two concepts arise out of radically divergent views of human nature, and they are mutually exclusive. *The inflicting of pain can never help us learn what we need to learn.* When the personal ego experiences pain, it immediately locks into a self-protective mode. The avoidance of more pain becomes the overriding issue, so moral or ethical issues simply disappear. If our aim is to help a child understand the issues, punishment is the worst thing we can do.

All members of a family are under the same laws of Life, no matter what their age. *Discipline is not something "big people" called parents do to "little people" called children. Discipline is our ongoing, reverent discovery of the transcendent principles of reality.* Life disciplines by being lawful, always and everywhere the way it is, no matter what our mistaken beliefs about it. Repeated frustrating attempts to make it conform to personal fantasies encourage us to stop telling Life what we want It to be and start asking It what It is and how It works. Then begins the fruitful and fulfilling process of discovering the spiritual nature of reality. The parents are presumably a bit ahead of the kids in their discoveries, so they appropriately take the lead in establishing the family patterns and structures that reflect Life's laws. They do so according to their highest understanding of those laws at the moment, knowing that forms will change as greater understanding takes place.

For example, a mother restricts ball-throwing to the outdoors because she values the beauty and order of the house; she sets mealtimes and encourages prompt arrivals by having the food ready, because she values these periods of family togetherness and sharing. Children can understand that the furnishings of the home are precious and that family meals are important, and they expect and want Mom to regulate these things for them. So if they happen on a given day to get so involved in a ball game or playing with a friend that they forget dinner time, they will feel sorry about it. They don't like to disappoint Mom and they are actually glad, though not necessarily conscious of it, that they have a structured home life. There is no reason to conclude that they are being deliberately disobedient or that they are inherently bad. Therefore, it is best to see it as simply a mistake and to make as little of it as possible. In this way we avoid that old devil, the Frankenstein reaction, which creates the monster of our innermost personal fears.

If we assume that children are consciously disobedient and seek to enforce our authority through punishment, we create the very thing we seek not to have: consciously disobedient children. Being treated as if they are deliberately disobedient little persons, children lose sight of their own innocence and play the role assigned. The importance of dealing with problems as issues in our own thinking is nowhere more clearly illustrated than in this fact. We have seen that love is the sorting out in thought of the child's quality identity from all personal misconceptions. It follows that accepting personal misconceptions and basing our behavior on them is unloving, and if unloving, then unintelligent as well.

We saw, with toddlers, that they are dominated by their own inner agendas. Even though older children are more aware of and responsive to externals, they too have their own issues. We all do, at every age. Friends and performance are important concerns to grade-schoolers. There are bound to be times when they are so distracted by their issues that it impacts on either school performance or home participation. Again, this does not mean that they are disobedient or bad.

But what about a child who seems consistently unresponsive to parental requests? Nick asked for help with his ten-year-old son, Kevin. He described the problem:

> There are times when Kevin just doesn't obey his mother or me. He refuses to respond when we tell him things. It builds up and it builds up until I can't take it any longer, and then I get physical. I come near to hurting the boy, and it scares both of us. That kind of rage and physical force isn't like me, and I just hate being provoked to that point. I don't know what to do. Should I let him know how angry I am the first time he doesn't respond, and not let it build up?

We discussed the issue on two levels, because parents' frustration is often so great by the time they come in that they cannot relax enough to think through beliefs until they have some behavior tools. We worked with the concept of "logical consequences."[8] Kevin does not pick up his toys after playing with them. What is the logical consequence of Mom or Dad having to pick them up? It is logical that Mom and Dad put them away, somewhere, so that they don't have to keep picking them up. After a while, Kevin doesn't have any toys to play with. Picking up his toys thus becomes his issue rather than his parents' issue. He picks them up so that he will have them to play with, not because Mom or Dad tells him to and punishes him if he doesn't.

Nick was concerned about his own feelings and reaction, and so we looked at the beliefs operating in his thinking. He said that Kevin "just had to have his own way" and then was embarrassed to discover that the same thought fueled his rage when Kevin didn't instantly comply with his requests. The human beliefs that operate in children's thinking are bound to be some version of their parents' beliefs. Often these are not beliefs that a parent cares to notice, so it requires some humility and openness on a mother's or father's part to own up to them. But as long as parents are attached to a particular belief about themselves or life, it will be very difficult, if not impossible, for their children to become free from it. If we really want our kids' problems to disappear, then we need to deal with the troublesome beliefs in our own consciousness, even if we must also take action in dealing with the child's behavior. The failure to face up to our own mistaken beliefs makes our attempts to force our kids to change abusive by nature. Every parent knows that a "do what I say but not what I do" stance is dishonest and therefore an abuse to a child's integrity.

Nick, fortunately, was able to recognize the part his thinking played in his problems with Kevin. It amazed him to discover that he and Kevin were both suffering from the same mistaken beliefs and not from each other. As Nick stopped seeing the situation interpersonally — "I've got to have power over Kevin's behavior" — he lost the sense of impotence that drove him to physical force. He could see that Kevin too could lose his rebelliousness if issues were discussed and explained, that is, if he were treated like a rational being instead of like an object that had to be forced into conformity. Nick then remembered noticing that when he had explained to Kevin why he had imposed a certain rule, the boy's belligerence had immediately dropped.

As parents, we have our own agendas, and when the children appear to disobey or be troubled, it hits hard at our "good parent" image. In our anxiety to prove ourselves, we may feel pushed to do something before we give ourselves time to understand. Then our children feel pushed rather than understood, and too often push-comes-to-shove. *Dis-*

cipline needs to start in our thinking. Employing the Fairy God-mother Principle is actually an exercise of parental self-discipline. When we learn to let truth discipline, that is, order and harmonize our own thinking, we find much less need for interpersonal management.

The Truth about Lying

It is during the early school years that the problem of a child's failure to tell the truth, or at least to tell the whole truth, surfaces. I know of no other single issue more infuriating to parents than that of a child's "lying." I put the term in quotes because the parental sense of what a child is doing is labeled with an ugly term that, from that moment on, obscures the parent's capacity to observe the issues. "Lying" in a parent's thinking is bad, wrong, unforgivable. Part of what makes it so reprehensible is the belief that it is done by the child's conscious, free choice.

Daphne's mother and stepfather were at their wits' end over the ten-year-old's propensity to lie, or at least to "fudge" on the truth. I asked for an example, and they provided one very typical of the problem.

> She has been told a thousand times where to put her bicycle. We have a path running through the backyard to the garage and storage shed. It's dark in back, and if something is lying in the path, somebody could get hurt. So the kids have very specific parking places for their bikes. But Daphne doesn't mind. And when she is caught, she lies.
>
> Yesterday morning, when we got up, we found her bike lying squarely across the path. When we confronted her with it, she said, "I didn't put it there." Can you believe that?! She is the only one who touches

her bike, yet she denied putting it there. When we just snorted and said, "Sure, the elves put it there," she then blamed her brother. "Maybe Charlie put it there." What can you do with such a kid?

At work here is a psychological mechanism called self-defense. Adults are just as subject to it as kids, but adults have developed more refined, sophisticated forms. When confronted with accusations of wrongdoing, how many adults say simply, "Yes, I am wrong. I apologize and won't do it again"? Most adults begin immediately to rationalize and excuse their behavior. Kids are just less adept at covering themselves.

When a child begins to develop a pattern of lying, it is usually a sign that there is a pattern of personal accusation on the parents' part. Of course, lying is not a good idea. But personal accusation feels like a threat to the personal ego, and it triggers automatically personal survival mechanisms. Denial is the most obvious defense, however irrational it may seem to the accusers. The very irrationality of it alerts parents to the need to come at issues in a less threatening way.

In Daphne's case, it was suggested that the principle of logical consequences be employed in dealing with the bike issue. If the bike is left in a place that is dangerous to the welfare of family members, then the bike gets put away where it is safe. But Daphne's defiance of parental directions also needs to be addressed, and it gives evidence that the parents have unwittingly fallen into a personal power mentality. Orders are being given by big people to little people, and little people are expected to obey just because the big people have said so. Invariably in such a setup, unless the little people are army inductees, they are going to resent being ordered about and are going to find more ways to circumvent orders than the big people can find orders to issue. And all the punishment in the world cannot really resolve this problem.

The Marvel of Spiritual Dominion

The marvel that heals the blame/punishment quandary is spiritual dominion. We need to feel that we can have dominion over our affairs and those of our children. This need is cruelly frustrated when we try to exert external control over people and events. Dominion is found in consciousness. It is not personal domination over persons, but the absolute dominion of the truth of Being over every false belief and false suggestion. We let our thoughts about a child be transformed by looking at that child through God's eyes.

Dr. Thomas Hora tells of a mother who came for help with her daughter who suffered from a phobic reaction to fire. The girl was terrified of even match or candle flames. The mother was asked, "What is the first thing you think of when you think about your daughter?" She was surprised to find herself saying, "Horses! She's just crazy about horses, and that's what comes to my mind when I think about her."

"It is interesting to note," said Dr. Hora, "that horses are terrified of fire." He then suggested that the mother contemplate her daughter's spiritual qualities every time she thought about her.

On the way home, the mother pondered her daughter's qualities. She was such an intelligent girl, so quick, so bright, so enthusiastic, so affectionate. The mother became lost in a loving contemplation of how delightful and gifted her daughter was. That evening, as she put candles on the table for dinner, her daughter said to her, "Mom, where are the matches? I'd like to light the candles tonight." And that was the end of the girl's fear of fire.

In this case, the mother found it easy to employ the Fairy Godmother Principle, because her daughter's problem didn't involve negative behavior toward her. It is always harder when we have our own personal reactions to deal with as well as the child's issue. Nonetheless, the positive fruits of spiritual dominion far exceed anything that personal manipulations can offer. Most of all, spiritual dominion lets us actualize the best rather than the worst of ourselves, and this is highly encouraging to us. Nothing makes a mother feel worse about herself than getting hooked into reacting to her child out of personal sense's worst garbage.

The First Step toward Spiritual Dominion

The first step is the refusal to accept either the child's personal definition of the situation or our own, personal definition as the truth of things. Some years ago I was required to write a paper on "knowledge" for a conference, and it enabled me to clarify this issue in relation to our boys.

> When one of our boys tearfully exclaims something like "You always let So-and-so do these things, but you *never* let me!" I am often astonished by the "knowledge." I don't know that at all. Quite the contrary, I know that this child is as justly and lovingly and intelligently and generously treated as any child could be. . . .
>
> Is my son what he knows himself to be: a poor, abused child? No. Is my son what I know him to be: a very fortunate child who thinks he's abused? No. He is what God knows him to be: not a child, not my son at all, but a consciousness, an individual manifestation of God's own awareness.

He may be distracted, at the moment, by an awareness of false beliefs which the world offers him about
life: littleness and bigness and fairness and unfairness
and all the rest. But if I can keep in mind that the issue is distraction, then I can, perhaps, keep from adding
to that distraction by lecturing him on the basis of my
own distractions: what a lucky boy he is, what a good
mother I am, how he should be more appreciative,
etc. Perhaps, instead, I can be still and remember that
neither his knowing nor my knowing constitutes the
reality of the situation. God only knows what's really
going on here.[9]

Asking ourselves what God knows about any situation
is the way to exercise spiritual dominion. For example, Erik
struggled greatly with his school work throughout the first
four grades. He was getting all the extra help the school
could provide, yet at one point his report card consisted
of straight D-minuses. This finally drove my husband and
me to take a stand in consciousness. Personal sense declared that Erik was like his dad, who had had academic
difficulties as a child. So we sought to see Erik from the
divine standpoint, in his spiritual rather than human identity. We acknowledged that intelligence is universal, not
personal, and so is not subject to beliefs like heredity or
personality. During the following week, Erik twice came
home from school with amazing stories involving math,
the subject that caused him the most difficulty. In both in-
stances, he had been called to the blackboard to do problems
and, despite his and the teacher's initial conviction that he
couldn't do them, he solved them promptly and properly.
From that time on, Erik's academic work steadily improved,
and he took several honors classes in junior and senior
high school.

Lawful Love

Our beginning years with our babies and toddlers yield an increasing sense of Life as a substance of positive qualities manifesting themselves in what is called, humanly, the growth process of child and mother. The crisis of performance invites an expansion of that sense to include a seeming external world of other people and structures. In this stage, the inclusive, nurturing mother-qualities expand out into the principled activity and expression of father-qualities. "Principle" means law, and the discovery of Love as having the absolute reliability of divine law is the marvel of the early school years. Like the mother in the riddle, we can learn that *we keep our loved ones safe and good not by possessing them but by releasing them to the operation of the divine law of Love.*

Just as fathers may discover their motherness in nurturing their babies, so mothers discover their fatherness as the children move out from under their nurturing protection. Mothering is essentially nurturing, and fathering is providing direction and empowering. These are expressions of love and law that, in God, are one: God's law is love and God's love is law, and it is to this principle or law of Love that we commit our children as they leave the home.

One Christmas season I took the boys shopping in a Christmas store. Each had three dollars in cash to pick out his ornament for the tree. I let them go off on their own to look around for a bit. A few moments later Erik was at my side, crying because he had lost his money. My first thought was, "I should have known better than to let him carry his own money. I should have known he would lose it." (Here we have a double-header in the blame game. He's to blame for being irresponsible and I for not anticipating it. This makes me feel bad and creates a strong urge to make him feel even worse.) We searched the store and asked everyone if they had seen the cash, but nobody had. On the way out of the store, I left our name and phone number with the cashier. She said, "Oh, nobody ever turns in cash," but she took the information anyway.

On the way home, I started to launch into a typical mother-lecture about the lesson in personal responsibility that this was teaching him. Suddenly the thought came: "But you can't have a silly, irresponsible little boy who is being taught a lesson and a world of divine Good where everything is safe and complete at the same time." I realized that we both had a lesson to learn, and it wasn't about personal responsibility. It was about omniactive Love/Intelligence. So I started talking with Erik about how this is God's world, not ours, and the law in God's world is Love, so things don't get lost or stolen. I said that we can expect the picture of lost or stolen money to dissolve as we pay attention to God's goodness instead of the lousy human picture of loss.

The next day, the cashier phoned to report that a mother had returned three one-dollar bills, saying that her child had found them in the store. The money wasn't important, but the proving out of the lawfulness of Good was inspiring and encouraging to our whole family.

Children's Safety Outside the Family

Nowhere is the principle of spiritual dominion more important than with regard to the other central issue of the early school years, namely, concern for our children's safety and integrity outside the family. We fear both physical harm and negative mental influence. We seem to live in a culture where children are at actual, physical risk in many situations that were formerly assumed to be simple and safe, such as walking to and from school and even being at school itself. Parents are concerned with how to teach their children what they need to know about avoiding contact with strangers without making them unduly fearful.

Safety does not lie primarily in external arrangements or saying the right words to our kids any more than discipline does. The seeming external world reflects back to us either the truth of Being or the personal beliefs we are cherishing. "As [a man] thinketh in his heart, so is he" (Prov. 23:7). The Frankenstein and Fairy Godmother Principles are as relevant with regard to safety as they are in relation to behavior. Thinking about what can go wrong tends to invite it.

In order to interact with others, positively or negatively, we have to be on the same mental wave length with them. The human misconception of life can be likened to a dream, and we participate, humanly, with those with whom we have "overlapping dreams." For example, people whose dream sense of themselves involves abuse or violence will find others who identify with these horrors with whom to act out the dream of life as abusive interpersonal interaction.

We cannot change the content of our dream identities to different dream identities. But we can relinquish the dream identity for the sake of spiritual identity, and this is the dynamism of spiritual dominion. *Dwelling mentally in the awareness of Life as essentially whole and good, we do not invite into our experience, or that of our children, the adversarial aspects of the personal belief level of thinking.* Psalm 91 describes the protective consequences of "dwelling in the secret place of the Most High," which is spiritual Consciousness.

Children Learn What They Live

The importance of learning to work things out in consciousness rather than in interpersonal interaction cannot be overestimated. It is a lesson that the parents must learn themselves and teach by example, since lectures about solving things peacefully are entirely ineffectual if the patterns in the home are personal and power-oriented. When potentially violent social situations arise, people react or respond according to the ways of thinking that have dominated in their families. If our children have learned to appeal to intelligence in situations of discord rather than to force, they will find ways to reason their way out of sticky social situations rather than having to punch their way out.

A Solid Basis for Making Decisions

Another very practical aspect of spiritual dominion is that it gives us a standard by which to make decisions regarding appropriate social situations for our children. "But So-and-so's mother lets him do it" are words designed to throw a mother into uncertainty, conflict, and even fear. It becomes increasingly difficult for mothers to know what is and is not good or appropriate, as the children get older and their contacts broaden. If there is one thing I have always hated, it is feeling caught between a child's heartfelt desire to do something and my own uneasy sense that it isn't quite right.

Tommy's best friend for many years lived two houses away. Tommy and Ben would be together all day long, in summer, and then often Tommy would ask to spend the night at Ben's house. We let him do so occasionally, but we didn't feel entirely comfortable with it. We would discuss it and often end up saying, "Well, I guess there's nothing really wrong with it," but it still didn't feel quite right. One day the thought came, "Okay, so there's nothing wrong with it. But is there something right with it? Is there any positive value in his sleeping over there all the time?"

This thought came like a shaft of sunlight, illuminating the entire scene. We discovered that *asking "What's right about this?" instead of "What's wrong about this?" brings clarity to any issue*. Looking for positive aspects of a situation, the negative ones came up more clearly by contrast. In this particular instance, we found no positive value in twenty-four-hour togetherness but immediately noticed that Tommy tended to become grumpy and tired, even after all-day contact with a friend, and tended to take it out on us when he first got home. Sleepovers only accentuated the problem. Since we value a clear and peaceful state of consciousness above all else, it was obvious that sleepovers, except in very special cases, were not called for. From that point on, decisions came out of asking the question, "What's good about this?" The boys did not like some of these decisions, but they accepted them with good grace when they saw that we had a reason for making them that was important to us.

When Other Adults Treat Our Child Unfairly

Increasingly our children come under the direction of other adults, and this can be a source of concern. One of the most difficult issues in this regard is what to do when children report that a teacher or coach is not treating them fairly. Our first impulse is probably to confront the individual and give him or her a piece of our minds. It really hits us hard when we think that a child of ours is being treated unjustly. But we do not want to react in a way that creates bad guys and villains.

I was very much helped in this regard by an incident that occurred when our boys were five and six and were playing Little League baseball. Tommy was on a team coached by a father who was a marine. This coach treated the little guys like they were new recruits and he was the drill sergeant. He tended to pressure and ridicule rather than positively encourage the boys.

Tommy's close friend Justin was on the same team.

Justin's mother was very upset about the way the children were being treated. Each time her son came off the field, she spoke loudly about how awful it was. Justin was soon in tears. I was becoming quite anxious and upset myself and was agreeing with Justin's mother that something should be done. But I noticed that Tommy didn't seem bothered, so I refrained from saying anything to him. Afterward I asked him if it bothered him the way the coach treated them. He said no.

Unable to let my upset go so easily, I said, "You really don't mind the way he hollers at you and orders you around?"

"Oh," Tommy said, casually, "that's just the way marines talk."

I felt a great weight of personal responsibility lift. This six-year- old boy had spontaneously discovered dominion in consciousness, and it automatically protected him from the coach's behavior. I didn't have to do anything except understand what my son was telling me. *Tommy did not suffer from the coach's harshness because he did not take it personally. In not judging and blaming the coach, he remained untouched by the coach's judgments and blame.* How did a six-year-old know this? It was clearly universal Mind's knowing. Many times children illustrate for us the truth that intelligence is universal. There is one Mind, not many minds, and the acknowledgment of one Mind is the truth that most potently addresses the multitudinous problems arising from the belief of many minds.

There is nothing wrong with discussing a seeming injustice with a teacher or coach, as long as our concern is clarification rather than blame. Often we will come out of such a meeting with a better sense of the other adult's issues, which can help us help our child. Human life is full of other people whom we may not like or agree with. Learning how to deal with such people is of great importance to our kids. Our maternal desire to rescue our kids from such difficulties is understandable but not necessarily helpful. Far better to share with them the secret of harmonious living — by taking our mental stand in the one Mind and its knowing, we can stay off the level of interpersonal adversarialness with its difficulties. This shows up as staying issue-oriented and knowing that *any issue can be resolved by universal Intelligence as long as we don't let it get misdefined as a matter of persons against each other.*

Children who turn automatically to intelligence rather than force for solutions have a much easier time with both their peers and other adults. Moreover, they grow up into adults who are not easily provoked into violence on the national and international scene. If we are concerned with world peace, we need to cherish peaceful homes and bless our children with a way of approaching problems that actually heals them.

Delighting in the Companionship
of Our School-Age Children

One of the primary delights of this period of motherhood is that the children become genuine companions. The wondering of the preschooler turns into the active interest of grade-schoolers in the larger world they are exploring. Family vacations are enhanced by the children's presence. They are old enough to take care of themselves yet are still mentally one with the family. They love to visit new spots, explore new activities, learn new things.

Part of what makes children of this age such good companions is that their mental, cognitive skills are rapidly developing now, just as their motor skills did in their preschool years. They really think about things; they begin to be able to reflect on Life in larger terms. We don't have to teach or preach to our children about Life, but this is a wonderful age with which to share our thinking, even our own questioning and searching. When we do this, we are respecting them as thinkers as well as stimulating them to think, and this lays a most useful foundation for parent-child dialogue in the teen years.

Our Discovery of Dominion
Becomes Our Children's Dominion

Hiking in the Sierras some years ago, we came upon a field of huge boulders, and the boys began to scamper over them. The parents of another child who was similarly engaged kept shouting to him to be careful: "Look out! You'll fall. You'll break your leg. Be careful. Slow down!" I shared their concern, but I remembered a testimony I had read in which a mother was doing spiritual study at the beach while her son climbed on an adjacent cliff. She saw him fall down the face of the cliff. However, her mind was so imbued with the truths she had just been reading that she heard herself calling out to him, "All is well" as he fell. He picked himself up, brushed himself off, and came over and sat by her side. He was fine, except for a few scrapes.

Even though I felt some desire to caution the boys, remembering this story I thought gratefully of Life's everlasting support instead. When the boys were finished and we hiked on, I shared with the boys my observations and thoughts. Parents often don't get feedback on such comments, and you never know if what you say registers at all. But later on, as we walked a narrow trail, Tommy remarked, "If you had to think about the dangers every minute, it would be awful. You'd be scared all the time." Learning that our thinking has a lot to do with what we experience encour-

ages kids to notice their thoughts. And this is the beginning
of spiritual dominion.

Because children are beginning to observe life in a larger
framework and to be vulnerable to the beliefs of others, it is
a good idea to have regular times of quiet discussion, when
things that may be bothering a child can come out spontaneously. You may notice tics or nervous habits arising during
these years. It makes us anxious to see our children anxious,
and the temptation is to nag about nervous habits or say
things like, "What is the matter with you?" This only makes
children feel guilty as well as anxious, which further im-
pedes their awareness of the troublesome belief. If we make
it a practice to handle our own anxiety by becoming aware
of Life's essential benevolence, this creates a mental climate
in which the child's fearful belief can surface. And if mother
and child are used to discussing their thoughts, the problem
will come out in conversation.

We need to discover our dominion in consciousness during these years, because our children need to discover their
dominion. *We are safe because safety is divine law, not because we
calculate to protect ourselves from personal danger. Our lives are
good because Life is already all the qualities of goodness, not because
we perform perfectly in every situation. Our appeal is never to
personal capacity — ours or our children's — but to universal principle.* We avail ourselves of the positive substance of divine
Life not by personal skill or achievement or merit, but by
acknowledging the spiritual facts of Being in consciousness.
This means that we can never be separate from whatever
resources may be needed.

The spiritual is the most practical level to work on, because spirit, by definition has no form. Any particular form,
by being what and where it is, is precisely not anything or
anywhere else. But spirit, being formless, is everywhere, all
the time, and can take any form. As humans, we all begin

with the idea that dominion means control over externals. Some of the time it seems as if we can have such control. But in the school of motherhood, personal management of our children and their affairs becomes increasingly painful to them and to us. *We are driven to spiritual dominion by our suffering, but we end up being gratefully drawn to it for love of the good we find in consciousness, when we seek to understand Life spiritually.*

ᲔᲐ

MOTHER'S RESOURCE GUIDE for Chapter 4

Meditations

THREE PRINCIPLES OF CONSCIOUSNESS

Take no thought for what should be or what should not be; seek ye first to know the good of God, which already is.

God helps those who let Him.

The understanding of what really is abolishes all that seems to be.

BEHOLDING THE GOOD

If we keep in mind what is really good, everything in our lives will be turning out good. It is important to have the right concept and the right understanding of what the good really is. Our experience in this world is but a shadow of spiritual reality. In order for the shadow to be good, the substance has to be clearly defined. What is the substance of reality? It is the intangible good which is in our consciousness. If the substance is clearly defined in consciousness, it casts a perfect shadow and to us it appears as good experience in daily living. But we must not be interested in the good of God primarily in the hope that it will pay off in material ways, because we are not then sincere seekers of the truth; we have ulterior motives. But if we are sincerely interested in knowing the real good, then, of course, we will be blessed in every way, even in the material world, because the material world is the shadow of spiritual reality.[10]

Game: Love Letter

Write a love letter to your child. This is especially good to do at a time when your child seems to be having difficulties, or you have difficulties with him or her. Think of what you love about your child. Bring to mind precious moments and special things about him or her and write lovingly to the child about them. Think of the child as being grown and gone from the home, and write the good things you would want your child to know about himself or herself.

You may or may not decide to send the letter, but in any case, keep it in your heart. In the next days, be especially mindful of the preciousness of the child's presence in your home and your life. Express your appreciation. Remember that we cultivate what we pay attention to, so cultivate the truth of your child, not the misconception.

Bedtime

This is often the nicest, closest time of the day with our active grade-schoolers. Besides talking together, reading to them, and adopting a bedtime ritual of Good-sharing is enriching. For years we sang together to the tune of the Tallis Canon:

> All praise to Thee, my God, this night,
> For all the blessings of the light.

(Here we would stop and share the blessings of the day.)
Keep me, O keep me, King of kings,
Beneath Thine own almighty wings.

Of course, after a while it became rote. The blessings were invariably listed as: "Salty-God-Jesus-and-the-angels-and-everything-we-did-today." (Salty was our dog.) So at that point we had to come up with some other way of listing the day's blessings.

Two Stories of Spiritual Dominion

1.

One of our four children . . . has had great difficulty in study and learning. In my busy household my mind was occupied with many things. [Recently] the child was struggling at the dining room table. He had started on his work sheet and it was awful; he was just gazing out into space and nothing was happening. So I stopped what I was doing and sat down at the table and didn't say a word, but just sat there. I was with him.

I have saved that piece of paper. The writing on the second half is completely different from the first. I didn't change it; I didn't say anything. On it is a note from the teacher that says, "Who did this?" Now, you see, I know it happens, but I don't know how, and I don't know how to repeat these things.[11]

This mother has experienced something for which she has no concepts. Something wonderful happened, but she doesn't know what, and she therefore doesn't have any idea of how to repeat it. She did not have even a God concept with which to work. So what was it that made such a difference in her son's work, even his handwriting? She said,

"I was with him." And the content of that pronoun "I" was more than she knew.

2.

In *Whole Child/Whole Parent* Polly Berends writes of another mother, equipped with a greater understanding, appealed to the "I" of Being in a conscious and specific way.

> Once my son came to me with a math problem that he could not solve. . . . He explained the problem to me, but my background was such that I couldn't even understand the problem. . . . Whom could we call that would know how? One call was made, but no one was home. "Anyway," my son admitted, "we're supposed to do it ourselves." Well, he could go to school and say that he had not been able to do it.
>
> But then realizing that there was no other mind to rely on I remembered the One Mind. I thought, he does not know how to solve this problem. I do not know how to solve this problem. But he does not have to rely on himself or on me or on anybody else. The only mind there is can reveal to my son what only it knows. "I have confidence that an idea for solving this problem will come to you," I said. "Let's sit down here and see." We sat at the kitchen table and waited. I read. In a minute he picked up his pencil. In another minute he shouted, *"Oh!"* and began to write furiously. When he came home from school the next day, I asked about the problem. Was his solution correct? Did any other students solve it? He answered yes to both questions. "But you know what?" he said. "I was the only one in the whole class who got it the short way."[12]

Testimony

One of my favorite bliss testimonies comes from an article that appeared in *The Atlantic*. It is by a woman named Margaret Montague and is entitled "Twenty Minutes of Reality." She describes the remarkable state of consciousness that occurred when she was recovering from surgery in a hospital. On a "dingy" March day, her bed was, for the first time since the operation, pushed out of doors to the open gallery of the hospital. She writes:

I cannot now recall whether the revelation came suddenly or gradually; I only remember finding myself in the very midst of those wonderful moments, beholding life for the first time in all its young intoxication of loveliness, in all its unspeakable joy, beauty and importance.... I saw no new thing, but I saw all the usual things in a miraculous new light — in what I believe is their true light. I saw for the first time how wildly beautiful and joyous, beyond any words of mine to describe, is the whole of life. Every human being moving across that porch, every sparrow that flew, every branch tossing in the wind, was caught in and was a part of the whole mad ecstasy of loveliness, of joy, of importance, of intoxication of life.

It was not that for a few keyed-up moments I *imagined* all existence as beautiful, but that my inner vision was cleared to the truth so that I *saw* the actual loveliness which is always there, but which we so rarely perceive; and I knew that every man, woman, bird and tree, every living thing before me, was extravagantly beautiful, and extravagantly important. And as I beheld, my heart melted out of me in a rapture of love and delight.... As for the interns in their white suits, I had never realized before the whiteness of white linen; but much more than that, I had never so much as dreamed of the mad beauty of young manhood. A little sparrow chirped and flew to a nearby branch, and I honestly believe that only "the morning stars singing together and the sons of God shouting for joy" can in the least express the ecstasy of a bird's flight.

Once out of all the gray days of my life I have looked into the heart of reality; I have witnessed the truth; I have seen life as it really is — ravishingly, ecstatically, madly beautiful, and filled to overflowing with a wild joy, and a value unspeakable. For those glorified moments I was in love with every living thing before me.... There was nothing that was alive that was not a miracle. Just to be alive was in itself a miracle....

Besides all the joy and beauty and that curious sense of importance, there was a wonderful feeling of rhythm as well. I heard no music, yet there was an exquisite sense of time, as though all life went by to a vast, unseen melody. Everything that moved wove out a little thread of rhythm in this tremendous whole. When a bird flew, it did so because somewhere a note had been struck for it to fly on; or else its flying struck the note; or else again the great Will that is Melody willed that it should fly.[13]

Such reports are like a peephole into Mind's awareness. These experiences occur when the personal misconception of the spiritual Universe drops away for a moment, and the individual directly perceives reality from the standpoint of the Divine.

As you read, let yourself linger over and savor the descriptive phrases that point so far beyond the normal appearances. They allow us to feast on the view of heaven itself. When I walk, I am mindful of such phrases as "ravishingly, ecstatically, madly beautiful" and "filled to overflowing with … a value unspeakable," and I let those ideas be a lens through which I see and think. If I am in some sort of mental funk, when personal sense says things look "gray" and "dingy," then I repeatedly remind myself that the "young intoxication of loveliness" is what is really present and is what my true identity is conscious of.

The positive effect of such meditations cannot be overestimated, for both mother and child. This is a form of "practicing the presence of God," and where God is present, everything negative and limiting and ugly is absent.

Recommended Readings

Dreikurs, Rudolph. *Children: The Challenge*. New York: Hawthorn Books, 1964. Excellent description of non-personal discipline. The concept of "natural and logical consequences" is very helpful.

Ginott, Hiam. *Between Parent and Child*. New York: Avon Books, 1969. I don't know of any recent book that is as practical and clarifying with regard to parent/child communication as this classic.

Chapter 5

TEENAGE

The Crisis of Respect /
The Marvel of Divine Integrity

Erik was lying on the beach, within hearing distance of two mothers who were surrounded by children. The kids ranged in age from about twelve down to preschoolers. The mothers were conversing rather loudly.

"How old is Melissa now?" asked one mother.

"She's twelve. She'll be thirteen in March."

"Oh, my God, can you believe it? She'll be a teenager!"

"I know. Isn't it awful? I dread it."

"Me, too. I don't know how I'll get through those years. What happens to kids? They turn into monsters!"

"She's already wanting to wear makeup. I just know she's going to be boy-crazy. All she wants to do is hang around malls with her friends."

"Poor you. Thank God I've got a few more years before teenage strikes!"

Overhearing this dialogue, Erik began to feel highly incensed. He was strongly moved to go over to the women, introduce himself as an ordinary teenager, and declare his innocence of monsterhood.

As I listened to this story, I felt torn. I certainly felt for Erik. He was a good kid, as friendly with adults as with his peers.

It was new in his experience to be negatively judged on the basis of age alone, and he felt hurt and outraged. Yet, dread is never far from the heart of the parent of a teenager, however exemplary the children, in part because of the culture we live in. So I could understand and identify with the mothers' concerns as well.

A Mother's Main Fears

A mother's two primary fears as she faces the teen scene are the loss of authority and the loss of affection. Even before the teen years arrive, we fear the possibilities pictured everywhere around us of beloved children turning into hostile strangers as their peer group becomes the center of their loyalty and values. Questions like these abound: "If I am not calling the shots, will something bad take over?" "If they are no longer dependent upon me, will my children still respect and love me?" But the teen years do not come in a vacuum. They are very much the fruit of the first twelve years. *The belief that puberty is a kind of magic wand that turns otherwise delightful children into a crazed and alien species is another one of those idiotic human beliefs that must be consistently refused admission into consciousness.* If we have understood that God is raising our children, and us along with them, then we will feel assured that God will stay on the job through the teen years, for all of us.

Fears Based on Misconceptions

Our fears of losing our authority and our children's affection are based on a misperception of what is taking place. We are not persons attached by human ties and vulnerable to the loss of some personal good as those attachments shift or dissolve. Life's agenda for the so-called teen years is the same as for any other period: living Itself to its fullest. Our teenagers are clearly blooming, but the cruel distortion of personal sense makes it seem that their blooming is our loss. This painful sense can make us miserable, or it can motivate us to look beyond the appearances and to gather our information from the universal rather than the personal standpoint.

The crises of the teen years require us to draw upon all that we have learned up to this point, and it helps to review the marvels that have healed the crises of the past stages:

1. The mother/child experience is the expression of the mother/child qualities of Being and not the interaction of two flawed fragments of life, called persons, trying to make a go of it with each other.

2. There is one Life. It is made up of all qualities of Good, and this Life lives us, in and as our consciousness. This (w)holiness is what is in charge of our living, despite and not because of the personal beliefs that we cherish. It is this Life, this "beauty of holiness," that we trust. It provides us with understanding and understanding supplies what is needed, practically. Nothing positive can be or needs to be forced.

3. The principle of this Life is Love/Intelligence. We and our children are not dependent upon personal, limited minds and capacities, nor are we personally respon- sible to run our lives, to get the good or prevent the bad. Dominion over our affairs comes in consciousness, where we relinquish personal control for the unerring and immutable control of the divine law of Good.

With our toddlers we learned to cherish understanding as that which controls behavior. With our grade-schoolers, we discovered discipline to be reverent responsiveness to Life's lawfulness. We can therefore look forward to the teen years with confidence rather than trepidation, because we have a firm foundation of universal principles to stand on.

Life is a treasure chest of limitless possibility. What we think of as the human life span is actually the opening up and gradual discovery of the precious, sparkling qualities that make up our true identity. Motherhood is a double discovery process: we get to explore our own treasures in new ways, and we share with our children their exploration. In fact, for many years we are the primary means through that they make their discoveries. *Every gem which we have helped our children discover and celebrate as the truth of their identity pays positive dividends for both us and them during the teen years. Great is our reward now for the Good-seeing and Love-seeing of the past.*

Parent-Teen Tensions

Parent-teen tensions center around issues of authority and respect. The human belief scenario may be illustrated by a family I saw only once but remember vividly. I had spoken with the mother over the phone. She described her son as negative and rebellious, in trouble at school and at home. He had been evaluated by a psychologist and deemed in need of therapy. Before the mother went ahead with that treatment, she wanted to consult a counselor who "believed in God."

Having been prepared for a considerably disturbed boy, I was pleased to discover a fairly typical young teenager. I spent quite a while talking with him about his situation and found him very much like one of our boys, who was of the same age.

Speaking alone with this boy's parents, it became clear that the problem lay much more in their expectations than in the boy. They were bright, disciplined young professionals, and he was their only child. The mother was a schoolteacher and expected academic excellence from the boy. The father was a controlled, ambitious man on his way up in some corporation. He expected a carbon copy of himself. Both parents focused a lot on the issue of respect, by which they seemed to mean "Yes, sir! No, sir!" responses. "He's just not respectful" they declared. I asked for an example.

"I can give you a perfect example," said the mother. "The other day he was watching television after school, which he's not supposed to do until he has done his homework. So I told him to turn it off. He did not do so immediately. I had to nag him and, finally, he grudgingly reached out with his foot and turned it off with his big toe!" She was clearly outraged. I laughed, because I could well imagine either one of my boys doing the same thing.

The father then repeated his charge that the boy was not respectful. I asked for another example. He replied that his son tended to bump into him, sort of push and shove, when they were together. Again I laughed. This was exactly the way our boys behaved with their father. I saw this as an expression of affection, much akin to the way a puppy bounds up and jumps on someone in its enthusiasm. But because the father interpreted this behavior as disrespectful, he could only condemn it.

Respect Arises in the Presence
of That Which Is Respectable

Respect can be a difficult issue between parents and teenagers. Underlying the insistence that "children should show respect to their parents" lurks the troublesome old interpersonal power/authority issue that first reared its head with our toddlers. Removing the respect mask, we often find the primitive and actually selfish belief: "My kid should behave the way I want him to, when I want him to." This sentence is riddled with mistaken beliefs that are the denial of everything Life has been showing us from the baby's birth on.

Respect is actually not a behavior but a state of consciousness that arises spontaneously in the presence of that which is respectable. It is a correlate to reverence. Reverence is our spontaneous response to that which is sacred: the divine, transpersonal reality. And respect is our spontaneous response to the qualities of the Divine manifested through an individual. *Our issue is not to get respect but to be respectable and respectful, that is, full of respect for the qualities that are the truth of Life. When we are full of respect, others will inevitably respect us. We not only don't have to insist on it, we cannot prevent it.* But the belief that other people are in this world to behave according to our personal dictates is not a respectful or reverent belief. It is not loving or intelligent. It therefore will not work and will cause us a lot of pain.

If we are having problems with respect, the first place to scrutinize is our own thinking and behavior, not that of our kids. We may notice, for example, that the parents of the "disrespectful" young teenager had not discussed the homework issue with their son. When I spoke with him, he indicated that he felt very tired when he came home from school and wanted to take a break before hitting the books. His parents had arbitrarily issued the edict of no TV until the homework was done. Is this a respectable decision? Would we, being refused the opportunity to have some input on a decision that affects us, consider it even just, let alone respectful?

With teens, just as with toddlers, it is a mistake to think of authority as vested in persons. When we think that way, we become concerned to keep personal authority over our teenager, and the personal power struggle kicks in. *Life, which has its own agenda, is the only Authority, and it is one to which both we and our teens are subject.* God does not raise our children according to our personal dictates, but according to his divine dictates. A respectful mental climate in the home must be based on our respect for Life's lawfulness rather than on personal behavior, and the law of Life is Love/Intelligence. *In drawing up guidelines for the home, we do not ask ourselves, "Who's the authority . . . me or him?" We ask ourselves, "What is loving and intelligent in this situation?"* It is loving and intelligent to discuss all structures involving teenagers with them. Neither we nor they are mind readers, though we often seem to expect one another to be. They cannot know how we think and feel about things unless we tell them, and we do not know how they are thinking unless we ask them to tell us. With regard to homework, one of our sons preferred to do it right after school so he could then be free, and the other felt a need for a complete change of pace until after dinner.

It Helps To Keep Our Eyes
on the Larger Unfoldment

Paying attention to the larger unfoldment rather than to momentary details can see us through some otherwise difficult issues. Teenage activities and behavior may not, at times, be respectable in our eyes. Moreover, the human developmental needs of teens do not enable them to recognize and respect their parents in the ways that we may crave. I remember commiserating with friends about the scathingly condescending tone of voice with which teens sometimes address parents. Learning not to take that personally is an exercise well worth our attention, since it can spare us many bruises to the parental ego.

Recognizing the non-personal unfoldment taking place, we find ourselves more able to smile, inwardly, at the teen's budding authoritativeness. Teens tend to be in love with their own thinking, believing that their discoveries about life are as brand-new to the world as they seem to them. A mother's role is to support that sense of authority, not argue with it and put it down because she knows so much more. We can support the new-found authority because we know that it is Mind's knowing and authority expressing itself despite and not because of that know-it-all kid. The support does not take the form of dropping all family structure and guidelines, but of a willingness to hear teenagers out on any issues that involve them. I often found my understanding of situations changing when I gave the boys the chance to tell me about them. Just because some activity didn't fit my old ideas didn't mean that it was necessarily bad.

For example, I was very uncomfortable with the boys' weekly attendance at teen discos, where they socialized with young people from all over the county. I thought they should be going to school dances and sticking with kids from their own school. When I fussed, I was informed that the theme park discos they attended were very tightly policed to prevent any alcohol, drugs, or fights. And, they said, the home parties that many of their school friends attended always included alcohol and sometimes attracted such hordes that the police were called. After that, I kept my mouth shut about staying in the neighborhood and was grateful that they knew their social scene better than I did.

My First Teen-Years Crisis

Perhaps the greatest crisis of the teen years for me came at the very beginning, at the time when I was subject to all the common parental fears and fantasies and had no actual experience with which to discount them. The incident involved our thirteen-year-old son lying to us and sneaking out with a friend and a bottle of wine to meet some girls. The scene contained all the ingredients sure to trigger a mother's teen-terror. A neighbor noticed the two boys hastily trying to hide the wine bottle as he passed and alerted us, whereupon my husband charged out and broke up the illicit gathering. I felt shocked beyond belief. Our son had deceived us, and it seemed a betrayal of monumental proportions. It seemed as if something terrible and inconceivable was happening. I reacted out of that sense, out of my own crisis, which did little to clarify the issues.

From the blessed distance of several years, I can now see that my shock was not due to his actions but to the interpretation I placed on those actions, based on my personal expectations. His behavior was incomprehensible to me because it was not something I would have done at his age, and I presumed him to be just like me. He could not verbalize his position to me then, and that only perplexed me more. But years later, as we talked about the incident — one, incidentally, which was of such amusement to one of the girls involved that she mentioned it when she signed his high school senior yearbook — the seeming mystery was revealed. He was in his first year of junior high school and had gotten from his best friend the belief that everything was somehow different in junior high. So he went along with the friend's suggestion, naively seeing it as a kind of harmless exploration of this fascinating new world. His shock at my reaction must have equalled my shock at his action!

Teen Ambivalence Yields
a Double Message to Parents

In retrospect, this incident reveals much about the adolescent sense of things, which, when understood and not taken personally, need not frighten us so. *It helps if we remember that this developmental stage is happening to and through our kids; it is not something they are doing to us.* Like the toddler, whose emerging sense of separate self is experienced as both threat and promise, teens are unfolding into a sense of having separate identities and lives, and this is both thrilling and frightening. They want our interest and support yet are liable to misinterpret it as meddling.

Fortunately, I remembered that as a teenager I had felt annoyed at my mother no matter what her response to my activities. When I had been out the night before, I both wanted and did not want her to ask me about how it went. This is a good example of adolescent ambivalence. If a mother asks, she is prying into a teen's private affairs. But if she does not ask, she is not interested and supportive. That's the way it felt to me. And I also remembered the ambivalence being compounded by the fact that I felt guilty about feeling annoyed at my mother. With such a stew-pot of emotions bubbling in a teen's consciousness, is it any wonder that their behavior seems at times incomprehensible?

A Parent's Initiative

At one point during our sons' teen years, my husband felt completely cut off from them. In earlier years, he had participated in their sports and school activities. But in high school, they seemed to him to be entirely self-absorbed in a world which spoke a different language and in which he was not welcome. Like many a parent before him, Jan went through a period of feeling hurt, unappreciated, and isolated from his sons.

Rather than sitting in his hurt and blaming the boys, however, it occurred to Jan that he could make an extra effort to show his interest in their activities. They were playing water polo and, though the games came at times that did not fit very well into his schedule, Jan rearranged his appointments so that he could attend. At first, the boys seemed oblivious to his presence and loath to discuss the games afterward. But by the third or fourth game, they began to chat with him on the sidelines and share the details with him during dinner.

This broke the spell of seeming isolation for Jan. He became aware of how important parental interest is to teens when it is a sharing interest rather than an authoritarian interest. And he also realized the importance of the parent being the one to take a positive step toward dissolving seeming barriers to communication. Dominion is ours, if we exercise it. We exercise it in our own thinking and behavior, not in trying to dominate our teens' thinking and behavior.

Problems Often "Come To Pass"

Many of the parents who have come to me for help with a young teenager required only the assurance that everything is actually all right. Children go through stages of fearfulness and negativity that can be considered normal. In a less sophisticated age we called the symptoms that arise during these stages "growing pains." *Problems literally come to pass, if we don't take them too seriously. Being present to children in an affirmative way often sees them through their troubled sense.* We can stay affirmative by employing the Fairy Godmother Principle, which reminds us that God takes care of our children by constituting the very truth of them and their lives. Therefore, keeping our eyes on that marvelous, divine Stuff of which they — and we — are made, is the most constructive activity we can undertake. Margaret Montague's celebration of "the mad beauty of young manhood" in her testimony at the end of the last chapter continues to give me fresh eyes through which to look at my sons and their friends.

It has surprised me to find a number of parents concerned about their teenager's lack of social involvement. A child who likes to read, who spends time alone in his or her room, who isn't outgoing, or who sticks with a friend or two of the same sex when others have started dating can be a source of worry to a parent. Unless there are gross signs of pathology, however, such behavior may actually be positive rather than negative. In our frantically interpersonal age, a late bloomer may be protected from many troublesome cultural pressures. It is our own insecurity that would deny to our young person the precious room to unfold at his or her own pace. Relieving our anxiety by doing our own work in consciousness rather than by pushing, nagging, and prodding our teenager helps us, as well as our child, get beyond the pressures of cultural fads. Paying attention to the spiritual qualities that are the truth of our teen is much more constructive that fretting over and picking at the personal details that annoy or worry us.

The Marvel of Spiritual Integrity

If it were possible to do that awful first teen crisis scene over, from the vantage point of the present, I would surely do it differently. But just as a new mother cannot possibly respond to her first infant's problems with the poise and understanding of an experienced mother, so a mother new to the teen scene can't expect herself to be a "cool mom." Genuine "coolness" — as distinguished from permissiveness — arises as we rediscover, in this new context, the trust and dominion of spiritual integrity. We then have the confidence to speak authoritatively and respectfully with our kids, being neither a patsy nor a tyrant.

Spiritual integrity is the oneness of Being. Integrity is defined as "the quality or state of being complete; unbroken condition." The integrity of Being refers to its unvarying wholeness. The growing assurance of Life's integrity arises our of the quality perspective on Life. *Human children seem to be constantly changing, different physically or mentally from moment to moment. Were that the truth of them, we would never know what to expect and would have no basis for assurance. But when we see qualities, we see the unchanging reliability of things, behind the surface differences.* The sweetness that so charmed us in the toddler is still there in the hulking teen; the creativity that we marveled over in the grade-schooler continues to delight us in the young lady. The recognition that these teens are our kids, whose positive qualities we know so well, and not some generic hunk of teenness, gives us the assurance that is based on the integrity of spiritual Life. The masks of personhood shift and change, but the integrity of quality Life knows nothing of the shifting. This discovery helps us to be reliable and consistent with our teens, which gives them a sense of an unshifting base from which to explore and discover.

Innocence and Purity Are Still the Truth of Life

Continuing to behold innocence and purity is of preeminent importance during the teen years, when personal sense most stridently declares the opposite to be true. When teens and young adults dress and look and behave in a way that most offends adult sensibilities, there is the greatest need for truthful seeing on our part. Keeping our vision quality-centered helps us and our kids through their periods of silliness and experimentation.

Recently a neighbor who is on the high school football team came home with a radical haircut. The entire team have their heads shaved at the beginning of the season as a kind of team badge. This boy, however, came home from the barbershop sporting a Mohawk. His father's reaction could be heard throughout the neighborhood. Screaming obscenities at his son, the father refused to let him in the house. The boy kept saying, in a steady voice, "Just let me explain." Eventually the father calmed down and allowed the boy inside. Later that day the boy came to our house to borrow something. I told him that I thought he handled his dad's reaction very well. "I'm going to shave the Mohawk off, though," he said. "I don't really like it myself. I just wanted to try it out for a day or two." I was struck with the simplicity and innocence of the boy's comment in contrast to the terror and violence of the father's reaction.

The more we take things personally and react on the basis of human fearfulness, the more we reinforce the false identity sense that is the problem. I have always prayed for my children by acknowledging that they are not children and not mine. They are consciousness, not person, and the Source of all consciousness is Mind. The human way of saying this is to say that they are here to work out their destinies with God, not with me. And I am here to work out my destiny with God, Life, not with them.

A Curfew May Respect Both Teens and Parents

A curfew always seemed to me to be a necessity. First of all, it gives kids a useful time structure. Teens find it virtually impossible to say to their friends that they simply do not want to do something or that they prefer to go home. A designated time to be home provides young people with an excuse for calling it quits that can be blamed on parents. The teens thus escape with their peer image intact. *As long as a curfew is reasonable and discussable, it is a service to teens that arises out of respect for their dilemmas, not a deprivation.*

Moreover, a mother who respects her children also respects herself and does not let herself be taken advantage of. A curfew was important to my peace of mind. Like many mothers, I didn't sleep well when the boys were out. If the return time was left open and I woke up before they were in, I wouldn't get back to sleep until they were home. This condemned me to long stretches of anxious uncertainty, and it condemned the boys to my consequent aggravation. Tom still teases me about the time — the 3 a.m. time, I always hasten to add — when I had the front door open before he even got out of his car. Avoiding such moments has been high on both the boys' and my priority lists, and a curfew proved helpful.

One Mind Is the Basis
of Parent-Teen Communication

It helps facilitate communication if parents share with teens the concerns that underlie the rules and account for their parental reactions. Realizing that there is one Mind helps dissolve the suggestion of an inevitable generation gap between teen minds and adult minds. Young people can understand that parents are bombarded from all sides with pictures of potential disasters and that it is therefore not a distrust of them as individuals that gives rise to parental concerns. In fact, we demonstrate our trust and respect for our kids by sharing with them our problems and needs with regard to their situation. They may even come up with alternative structures that better meet the needs on both sides.

From conception through the first few years, love and nurture are inclusive, surrounding and supporting the child qualities. With the school years, the inclusiveness begins to yield. In the teen years, the substance of loving support does not change but assumes different forms. The love that physically sheltered in the first months now expresses itself in allowing our children privacy and room for their own explorations. Support is for the expansion and maturation that are taking place.

Life's Integrity Heals Our Possessiveness
Because It Heals Our Fear

Giving our teens both support and space requires the releasing of personal possessiveness, and this is not really possible until we have found the basis for their safety in the integrity of divine Life. The hazards facing our teenagers these days are terrifying to parents. I had qualms about the forms of our boys' social activities at every point where they were different from my own experience. And the discrepancies were frequent and substantial. I often thought, "Give me a break! My idea of a great Friday night was four of us girls gathering around the piano and harmonizing away at folk songs. A horde of pomade-haired, Drakkar-drenched, gnarly dudes heading for a night abroad in Orange County takes some getting used to!" But at each point, when I took the time to discuss their activities with them, I came away reassured about their choices.

As mentioned before, the boys used to go to local theme parks that featured teen discos. They and their friends became quite proficient at synchronized group dancing. They often ran into other groups of dancers who came to compete, and these informal competitions sometimes ended up with ill will, to the point of invitations to "meet in the parking lot afterward." In every instance, the matter was resolved without violence. Since a fight was not considered an option, they always found some way to defuse the situation and often ended up shaking hands with the other guys.

Sex, Drugs, and Cars —
A Parent's Trinity of Terrors

Our fears about our teenagers focus on sex, drugs, and cars because these are where the greatest dangers lie. But the quality of consciousness that a kid brings into the teen scene is more important than any aspect of the scene. And their quality of consciousness reflects our consciousness of their quality identities. *Keeping our attention on the reliability of the divine qualities that are living our kids provides a stable foundation in consciousness that acts to neutralize toxic influences from the culture and peer group.*

Even though I faced the teen threats with the same trepidation as any parent, they did not turn out to be the problems that they could have been, had the threats been taken seriously. Franklin Delano Roosevelt's famous statement, "We have nothing to fear but fear itself," is a universal truth. It is fear that activates the Frankenstein reaction, in which we end up creating the very monsters we try to prevent. The Fairy Godmother Principle, which is nowhere more important than with teenagers, works because it refuses to start from a basis of fear. Taking our stand with God, we are able to face down the monsters, and a monster faced is a monster disarmed. "If God is for us, who can be against us?" (Rom. 8:31)

Again and again, I gratefully marvelled as my sons found their way through the potential pitfalls of the teen years without major difficulty. I had the same sense as in their infancy, of something within unfolding out with its own unerring direction and positiveness. Problems passed quickly, and each boy became increasingly centered and creative.

Alcohol and Authenticity

One of the most troublesome and fearsome issues with teens is the use/abuse of alcohol. Of course, all drugs are a dreadful problem. But even the kids who wouldn't dream of doing other drugs are susceptible to alcohol. I was both amused and grateful to notice that one son got caught twice during high school when he tried drinking beer. In the first instance, school authorities caught and disciplined him, and in the second case, the police gave him a ticket. He — and we — were required to attend a workshop on drug and alcohol abuse.

When my husband and I found ourselves "in the lineup" with the other parents, we realized that we needed to be clearer about our position on alcohol. We could not forbid the boys to drink beer. We have never operated that way with them. But we did discuss the issues and make clear that we do not approve of illegal behavior, and we consider alcohol consumption singularly troublesome. As long as they live at home and we are legally responsible for them, we expect them to obey the law.

It is important that parents be authentic in discussing such issues with their teens. Alcohol is such a great problem in our culture because it is a highly cherished substance in general. Tom told recently of a fraternity workshop in which the boys were counseled about the dangers of alcohol, and a chapter that had banned its use entirely was greatly praised. But that evening at the banquet the alcohol flowed freely at the head table! Alcohol is as troublesome to adults as it is to teenagers. We cannot lecture them about its dangers and then guzzle it in their presence. Teens spot such inauthenticity instantly, and it makes them appropriately cynical.

Beware of "Good" Human Advice

We cannot feel assured about our kids' well-being on the basis of anything that's visible to human sense. The impression we get from even positive human approaches to problems like alcohol is that any young person is susceptible and parents must be alert at all times, because they will be the last to know about their child's problem. This may be true, humanly, but it borders on activating the Frankenstein Principle. Fear of our kids falling prey to drugs must not become a focus of consciousness because that blocks the divine, quality Life from our awareness. It is the misconception we want to lose sight of, not the Good. We must beware of such good human advice because it arises from a too-narrow viewpoint on the situation.

When concerns come to mind, we protect our children by acknowledging that "it is He that hath made [them] and not we ourselves" (Ps. 100). We spoke in chapter 1 about the baby bringing with it an angel. This is a nice concept to remember any time we are concerned with what is "having charge over" our kids. I once read a father's moving story about his son's drug addiction. For a time, no communication seemed possible between father and son directly. So the father had what he called conversations with his son's angel. Eventually the boy was healed. Though the father never defined what he meant by "angel," his focus of attention was clear. He refused to believe the picture of a drug addict and kept being mindful of the truth of the boy's spiritual identity until the truth dissolved the personal picture.

Most parents have had their own problems with smoking, drinking, drugs, and/or sex. We would like to be able to pass on what we've learned to our kids, so that they don't have to learn things the hard way. It does seem, though, that they have to learn through their own experience, however clichéd that may sound. But what they experience and how they learn is greatly influenced by their state of consciousness.

Knowing What's Right Is More Important Than Knowing What's Wrong

It is not nearly so important for teens to know what is wrong, harmful, and dangerous as for them to know what is right, good, beautiful, true. It is our awareness of the qualities of Life that sorts through the possibilities and temptations that confront us and determines what we end up considering to be good and thus choosing. *Knowing something of the real Good, our kids are not nearly so vulnerable to the supposed goods of teen society.* If we would fill our schools with qualities education — that is, education in the qualities of real Life — as well as teaching the facts about sex and drugs, teenagers would be less likely to grab for self-destructive goodies out of an ignorance of where true satisfaction lies.

Sexual Miseducation

The need for familiarity with the spiritual qualities that make up the ultimate good of Life is nowhere more important than with regard to sex. I am astonished to see how many scenes of sexual intercourse bombard our children on TV and movie screens. This is a far more significant form of sex education than all the hygiene lectures ever devised. Sexual intercourse, specifically, is repeatedly portrayed as *the* appropriate behavior to express positive interest in a person of the opposite sex. It precedes even getting acquainted or, perhaps, is seen to be the primary way of becoming acquainted. There seems little interest in waiting to discover if the people share common interests and values, let alone being committed to building a life together.

This portrayal of sex as the ultimate good of a relationship is miseducation. For me, the real problem with it is that preoccupation with sex acts as a significant barrier to the discovery that the good lies not in body or personhood but in the consciousness of Life as the wholeness of spiritual Good. *Sexual activity actually is not a good in itself. It very much reflects the qualities of the individuals participating in it.* The more we have participated with our kids over the years in the discovery of Life's completeness and of the good as an issue of quality rather than sensory indulgence, the more their dawning sexuality arises within the divine context that alone can sanctify and protect it.

The way to enjoy quality sex is to be more interested in qualities than in sex. If parents understand and live Life from a spiritual standpoint, their children are imbued with that sense of things. Though they may go through periods of trying out the world's offerings, they cannot ever lose their underlying spiritual orientation. A spiritual perspective makes the best possible invisible family heirloom.

Spirit Maintains the Integrity of Both Teens and Parents

We respect our kids' need to learn from experience, but at the same time, we respect ourselves and what we've learned. We share with them our thinking. Perhaps most importantly, we maintain the integrity of the home. One of the reasons I wanted our boys to go away to college is that I know they need to be free to make their own discoveries, and I cannot give them that freedom while they are residing at home. Adolescents need to separate, to distinguish themselves from parental identity. Being clear and consistent about our values gives teenagers a stable backdrop against which to make their necessary explorations.

The Larger Viewpoint Is a Source
of Healing Humor

When parental integrity is rooted in the givenness of Life, which was the marvelous discovery of our first years as a mother, then we find that the adolescent separation process can take place without major discord. It has been my experience that kids can get the adolescent development done without seeing parents as adversaries. I have loved noticing how each boy has handled the human sense of needing to make distance. As a family, we have profited greatly from a capacity to laugh at ourselves, and both boys have used humor to break up moments of tension between us. Every time one of the boys would reply with humor instead of hostility to some instance of my mother-stuff, I would be grateful. We have all been spared much stress because of this blessed humor.

Verbalizing and laughing about the inevitable teen-parent friction points, the family set-ups, and personal idiosyncrasies takes all the steam out of them. A friend responds to a teenage son protesting something she has said, "Look, Kenny, that's just my mother-tape running itself. I can't help it. You just have to be patient with me." Every family spontaneously develops its own jokes and rituals for handling daily interaction. The important thing is not to take any of our personal stuff too seriously. Humor comes more easily and naturally when we have all along seen through the pretentious self-importance of personal sense. I long ago discovered in counseling that people's inability to laugh, even ruefully, at themselves and their problems indicates a poor prognosis for counseling success.

Laughter is the release, in consciousness, of the complete attachment to the human belief that is the problem. Laughter is healing because it springs from a standpoint that puts the situation in a larger perspective than that of the personal ego. I once read a testimony of a woman who was on her deathbed with relatives surrounding her. As she began to pass on, her young daughter piped up in a childish voice with some comment about her appearance, which struck her as funny. She started to laugh and couldn't stop. Pretty soon everybody in the room was giggling uncontrollably. She not only didn't die, she was soon completely well.

Personal Ego Is the Source of Seriousness

What makes parenthood seem deadly serious to some parents is the personal responsibility belief. When we find ourselves feeling very serious, it is evidence that we have let personal ego sense take the throne in our thinking. It always causes trouble. Even humanly we shy away from those who, we say, "take themselves too seriously." When that little ego thinks it has to be the mother or father, it sets itself up to take everything about the child's life and behavior personally. Kids then have no room to make mistakes or have problems because parents feel blamed for the trouble.

As a young teen, one of our boys was suffering from a physical problem that a psychiatrist told me was psychosomatic and was due to his anger because I didn't love him properly. The boy supposedly felt that I favored his brother. Despite the transparent folly of this belief — what kid with siblings doesn't feel this way, at times — my pride was pricked, and I fell for it. For twenty-four hours, personal sense had a heyday, producing such thoughts as "If my love for my son is so inadequate as to make him sick, he would be better off if I were dead."

After a day of self-torture, truth came blessedly surging into consciousness: "There is no human mother and no human son. God is Father/Mother and Son. There is no human love, only divine Love, which is universal and perfect." The unbearable weight was lifted. I was not responsible for my son's well-being. My love was not poisonous, because God's Love is the only Love there is. I didn't have to be the perfect human mother after all.

A few days after this, the boy unwittingly revealed his own version of the terrifying belief that he was personally responsible for perfectly managing every detail of his life. We were meditating together, using the form of "talking with your angel." I asked him what he would like to ask his angel, and he replied, "I would like to know what to do to digest my food properly." As we then sat quietly together, the sense of personal responsibility implied in his question struck me forcibly and humorously. I said, laughingly, "You don't have to know how to digest your food. Your body knows exactly how to do it. Who do you think you are, to try to take over the job your body was created to do perfectly?" His face suddenly lit up with a smile, and I could tell that the fearful spell had been broken. Sure enough, his physical problem disappeared rapidly after that.

Transpersonal Oneness with Our Children

We start out one with our children mentally, and that is good and important to their welfare. As the children grow, that initial mental oneness needs to lose its personal, psychological aspects and be transformed into the recognition of the oneness of divine, universal Mind, Life, Love. Spiritual integrity means that I am one with my children in consciousness rather than interpersonally. The qualities that make up their true, spiritual identity are the same qualities that are the truth of my own identity.

Our human sense of identity always limits and excludes many qualities that are actually always ours because they are Life's. *Life is everything that it is wherever it is. Just as there cannot be dry water or cold, dark sunshine, so there cannot be a manifestation of Life that does not include all of Life's characteristics.* All the qualities of femininity and masculinity, motherness and fatherness and childness, which appear to be scattered around outside of us as other people, are the truth of what we are. Our spiritual oneness with our children never changes, even though their size, shape, and proximity do.

Parent/Teen Discomforts Can Be Gifts

The teen years offer us the gifts that facilitate the transition of the kids to their own independent living and of us to less material and personal forms of motherhood. Just as our nine months' pregnancy readied us for the crisis of becoming Mother, so the gradual development of the children's independence and maturity over the teen years gives us ample opportunity to transcend personal possessiveness in the discovery of the universality and omnipresence of Good. Many women find new directions of activity, from job opportunities to gardening to volunteer work, unfolding spontaneously as the children take up less time and attention.

The very discomforts of this period, for both parents and kids, help dissolve the mental attachments, as Life intends. Our children need to break out of what one counselor calls "the family romance." They have the positive impetus of their developmental stage and the promise of the new delights of freedom pushing them out. For mothers, the breakup of the family romance feels negative. Motherhood was difficult at points, but the sense of being a family made it all worthwhile. "What's in it for us as our kids move on to their own lives?" we wonder.

It helped me to notice that the family romance was already broken by the last couple of years in high school. Our children no longer share our lives. Motherhood is very rewarding, humanly, as long as we and the children share a life, so that what we do for and with them is ours at the same time. Vacations are more fun for us because the kids are there. We love to see them well-clothed, to provide them with a lovely home, to welcome their friends, because it all enhances our own living. But motherhood becomes decidedly less personally rewarding when the kids need to use the material and financial and emotional resources in ways that separate them from the home and family life. That's why it is so important to have developed the transpersonal sense of motherhood throughout the early years.

I found that while school was in session the basic family structures remained somewhat intact. But summers edged toward what seemed like chaos, with the boys often working until midnight and socializing even later on nights they didn't work. My husband and I are early risers and I am early to bed. So I encountered the boys only briefly, as they staggered groggily from their beds at lunchtime and dashed off to work in late afternoon. The messy rooms, dishes left in the sink, late night phone calls, hours behind closed doors of bathroom or bedroom perfecting their personhood or giggling over girls, all provided me with increasing willingness, even eagerness, for the boys to operate from a base other than my home.

I was grateful to have a positive impetus as well. Because my own college years away from home were so important to me, we had always planned for our sons to go to college and live on campus. There was much sharing in and enjoyment of the exciting process of exploring colleges and a joint thrill in the discovery of what seemed to be the right ones.

Young people need parents' support in the anxiety-producing process of taking college entrance exams, applying to and being accepted or rejected by the universities of their choice. The kids tend to be very single-minded about their choices once they have made them. Parents, having a broader perspective, can provide reassurance that Life unfolds itself unerringly, whether or not we get what we want at any given moment. Though one son did not get accepted by the college of his choice, the college that offered itself turned out to be perfect for him. He probably learned more by that experience than did the other son who got the college he wanted. With both boys, the unfolding of college plans involved a very rewarding sense of joint participation in the Good. The pain of loss is more than compensated by the gratification of seeing children developing the independence and assurance so necessary to their happiness and maturity.

Outward Bound...

When Erik was sixteen, he went to a three-week Outward Bound Leadership School in the Sierras. He had a rough and marvelous time. At the end, he was assigned to lead a group of a half-dozen kids on a three-day final expedition. When his group leader gave him the assignment, he felt shocked. "There is absolutely no way I can do this," he thought, as he wandered off in a state of panic. Then came another thought: "Has Life ever, in all my years, left me completely in the lurch? Have I ever just gone down the tubes?" He saw that the answer was no and the next thought was then inevitable: "Well, then, I can expect that this time it won't happen either."

He gathered the group together, and they decided on an expedition motto: "Do it with style." Though tears of self-pity and fear ran with his sweat during the first day's hike, by evening the little group had managed to reach their first destination. The next two days went increasingly better and they finished their assignment on time and even did it "with style" by climbing an extra peak along the way.

When I heard Erik's account of his final expedition, I felt very humble and respectful. "Who's the authority here?" I thought. He had actually lived out — had been courageous enough to test out — the reliability of Life, which we had so often talked about through the years. His experience has become a guideline for me. If he could face his fears and move on in his recognition of divine support and guidance, can I do less?

Motherhood's High School

The teen years are motherhood's high school. We, like our children, find the lessons more demanding because we are capable of higher-level work. The issues are not different from those of a decade earlier, but they come in seemingly more complicated and intense forms. Just as we wouldn't let our high schooler get away with complaining because algebra is harder than beginning arithmetic, so we need not complain that it's harder to mother a fifteen-year-old than a five-year-old. The sense that insists that it was more fun or easier or more rewarding when they were small is the same sense which, when they were small, moaned and groaned over interrupted nights and earaches and toilet training. *Now, as then, the real challenge and joy of motherhood is not in the details of daily management but in being consciously present to the wonder of Life's Self-manifestation.* Noticing Love and intelligence, creativity and vitality, spontaneity and playfulness manifesting themselves in teen form and teen-mother form is an activity of ceaseless delight.

ᴥ

MOTHER'S RESOURCE GUIDE for Chapter 5

Wisdom and Knowledge

Call unto me, and I will answer thee, and show thee great and mighty things which thou knowest not. (Jer. 33:3)

Cultivate a desire to know the things of the Spirit, make the getting of wisdom a passion; welcome each new thought as though it were the first that you had ever received; try to find a lesson in every experience, expect a message from each one you meet, make an effort to see from the other's point of view; *and be meek* — meekness is the only soil in which spiritual knowledge will grow.

The wisdom that is from above is first pure, then peaceable, gentle, easy to be entreated, full of mercy and good fruits, without doubtfulness, without hypocrisy. (James 3:17, ERV)[14]

Being wise parents doesn't mean being know-it-all parents. Rather, it means being eager learners ourselves. Loving "the wisdom that is from above" ourselves encourages our young people's interest in the larger issues of Life.

Two Stories of Mother Wisdom

1. JOINING THE CHURCH

A minister's wife in Scotland told the following story. Her older boy, Robin, had reached the age to be confirmed in the church. Being the son of the pastor, it was expected that he would do so. But he refused, and when his parents tried to talk with him about it, he had nothing to say.

One evening, he and his mother had a little spat. She spoke harshly to him, and he ran upstairs and locked himself in his room. Reviewing the incident in her mind, the mother concluded that she had been at fault. She went to her son's room, knocked on the door, and said, "Robin, I just want to apologize. I was wrong to say what I did, and I'm sorry." Then she went back downstairs.

A bit later that evening, Robin came down and spoke with her. He said, "Mum, I've decided I want to join the church. The reason I wasn't going to was that adults always seemed to act like they know everything and are right all the time, and children are always wrong. And that didn't seem fair or truthful. But when you apologized just now, I realized that you don't think that way. So I think I'd like to join the church after all."

Robin's refusal to join the church had nothing to do with the church. It had to do with his sense of not being respected by adults. So many specific issues with teens aren't really about the issue but are about the teens' sense of themselves and of how their parents think about them. There is nothing to be lost and much to be gained in talking with our teens as if they are intelligent and respectable human beings, just like us!

2. PLAYING IN THE RAIN

Doris had had problems over the years with her son Jeremy. But she had been able to see that his seeming rigidity and re-activeness was a reflection of her own rigid way of demanding the behavior she wanted from him. She had learned a thing or two over the years. So, when there came a warm rainstorm, one day when Jeremy was a young teenager, Doris was able to respond rather than react.

When her son went outside without his jacket, Doris checked her impulse to holler at him that he had to put it on. She thought, "He's old enough to know whether or not he's cold." She watched out the window as he and his friends romped and splashed in the rare Southern California rain, and she actually enjoyed seeing them getting wet.

When Jeremy and his friends came in for a food-and-TV respite, Doris simply tossed them towels and told them to stay off the sofa. After a bit, they went back outside, where they proceeded to get thoroughly soaked. Doris went out to run an errand. Seeing the boys' delight in the water play, she was struck with an idea. She rolled down her window and called Jeremy to her. He came reluctantly, obviously expecting to be scolded and sent inside to dry out. Instead his mother said to him, "Why don't you and your friends line up on the curb by that big puddle, and I'll drive by and give you a real splashing?"

For a moment, Jeremy stared at her blankly, then gave a whoop and ran off to tell his friends. They lined up at the edge of the curb while Doris drove through the massive puddle not once, but three times. She then drove off on her errand, leaving three dripping, yelping boys, dancing around with delight. Her only thought, she reported, was, "What will the other boys' mothers think when they hear about this?"

Meditation: An Enlightenment Testimony

The following excerpts are from an account of one woman's profound "satori" experience, which came after many years of Zen Buddhist study and meditation. It has been a favorite focus of meditation for me, one which I have used so often over the years that I know these passages by heart.

A deep happiness was there.... Slowly my focus changed: "I'm dead! There's nothing to call *me*! There never was a *me*! It's an allegory, a mental image, a pattern upon which nothing was ever modeled." I grew dizzy with delight. Solid objects appeared as shadows and everything my eyes fell upon was radiantly beautiful.

These words can only hint at what was vividly revealed to me in the days that followed:

... The least expression of a weather variation, a soft rain or a gentle breeze, touches me as a — what can I say — miracle of unmatched wonder, beauty and goodness. There is nothing to do: just to be is a supremely total act....

I feel a love which, without object, is best called lovingness. But my old emotional reactions still coarsely interfere with the expressions of this supremely gentle and effortless lovingness.

I feel a consciousness which is neither myself nor not myself, which is protecting or leading me into directions helpful to my proper growth and maturity, and propelling me away from that which is against that growth. It is like a stream into which I have flowed and, joyously, is carrying me beyond myself.[15]

This beautiful statement lucidly communicates the sense of things that constitutes spiritual Consciousness. The ordinary human griping about the weather falls away in exquisite wonder. Human romance gives way to objectless, "supremely gentle and effortless lovingness." Belief in an external God becomes a benevolent Consciousness that is the truth of one's own knowing. It is "not myself" because it is not personal, but it is not other than "myself" because it is my divine identity, carrying me beyond the limits of personal identity sense.

Chapter 6

YOUNG ADULTHOOD
The Crisis of Loss /
The Marvel of Divine Completeness

When "the Day" came, Erik and I loaded his belongings into the car, and I drove him to the university campus, thirty miles from home. I helped him move into the dorm, and we talked about setting up his bank account and getting his phone installed. I drove him to the cafeteria for lunch and decided not to stay, though a number of parents were eating with their students. There seemed no point in prolonging the leave-taking.

I parked the car and got out to give him a goodbye hug, saying, "Be sure to let me know your phone number just as soon as the phone is installed." We hugged briefly ... I could feel a wave of emotion from his side as well as mine. I drove off.

As soon as I hit the freeway, I started to cry. I knew I could work with the feelings, but it seemed appropriate to let them have their say. I was surprised to find that the words that came to mind through the tears were not only, "I want my baby," but equally, "I want my mommie." I felt as much an abandoned child as an abandoned mother.

I was surprised by the magnitude of the feelings of loss after I delivered Erik to his campus home. They were much

150

greater than anticipated and much greater than the situation warranted. For the first few weeks, every time I would do laundry or grocery shopping, I would get teary. Buying food for two instead of four and doing the seemingly infinitesimal wash of two adults compared with the loads produced by teens were accompanied by strong feelings of loss. Buying hamburger roles at the bakery where I had for years bought four, the question came up. "Only two this time?"

"Yes, only two. My boys have gone away to college." Sob.

When I put it to myself: "Would you honestly rather be doing huge washes and cooking for four?" the answer was a resounding "No." But that, clearly, wasn't the issue. It had something to do with the loss of the value of doing these mundane things that motherhood provides. Though I told myself that I was now free to cook what my husband and I like without having to cater to teenage tastes, I had a hard time being interested in cooking at all.

The Universal Crisis of Un-becoming a Mother

It seemed as if I had tapped into a sort of archetypal mother sense. What human mother does not agonize over separation from her children? Many of my neighbors and friends, whose kids were just going off to college, were likewise having a hard time of it. Primitive societies give ritual structures for working through such transitions, but we sophisticated Western women have to work it out on our own. It helped me to see that I wasn't suffering from a personal drama but was experiencing a phase of the universal human drama. Anne Morrow Lindbergh's description of her crisis is clarifying:

> When I wrote *Gift From the Sea*, I was still in the stage of life I called "the oyster bed," symbol of a spread-

ing family and growing children. The oyster bed, as
the tide of life ebbed and the children went away to
school, college, marriage or careers, was left high and
dry. A most uncomfortable stage followed, not sufficiently anticipated and barely hinted at in my book.
In bleak honesty it can only be called "the abandoned
shell." Plenty of solitude, and a sudden panic at how
to fill it, characterize this period. With me, it was not
a question of simply filling up the space or the time. I
had many activities and even a well-established voca-
tion to pursue. But when a mother is left, the lone hub
of a wheel, with no other lives revolving about her, she
faces a total re-orientation. It takes time to re-find the
center of gravity.[16]

Like Anne Morrow Lindbergh, I had expected my work
to fill in the gap when the boys left. But it is not a matter of
filling time. The void that one feels is a mental void, not a
durational one. A mother is a mother preeminently in consciousness, and it is here that the emptiness is experienced.
I was used to being mentally in touch with my kids all the
time, even when they were off on their own activities. My
day, for nineteen years, had been absolutely determined by
and had revolved around their presence, their needs. When
Tom had left the year before, I had had a very unpleasant sense of mental vacuum in relation to him for the first
few weeks. But he came home fairly frequently, and Erik's
presence kept my daily routine virtually the same.

With both boys gone, I felt completely at loose ends.
When I would call and leave a message on the boys' answering machines and they would not call back within a few
hours, I felt uneasy, even agitated. There was a sense of being
disconnected from some part of myself, with a consequent
urgency to hook up in some way.

As I observed my thinking carefully, it became clear that the crisis was not in the physical absence of certain persons. In fact, a mother may experience this crisis while a child is still living at home. A son's first serious girlfriend or a daughter's first summer job away from home, for example, may give rise to the sense of loss that constitutes the crisis.

The latter teen and young adult years have not been my favorite period of motherhood by any means. The boys' lifestyles conflict significantly with mine, and it is not a lot of fun sharing a house with them right now, as much as we all do our best to accommodate one another. So the problem was not that they were not right here, under foot. It was rather a personal crisis, one involving who I am, who life is going to let me be. Mother is, in Anne Morrow Lindbergh's apt image, the "hub of a wheel with ... other lives revolving around her." The question that comes up is: "Who am I, then, when no other lives revolve around me? What is a hub without the wheel?" The flip side of our initial crisis — the acceptance of a new identity — is the seeming loss of identity when the ingredients supporting it are gone. If motherhood were just a role rather than an identity, the shift would not seem so radical.

Re-evaluating One's Purpose, Meaning, Worth

During the active mothering years, we never have to ask ourselves what we are going to do today. We are not prone to wondering what our lives are all about. In the seeming mental vacuum which followed Erik's move, I found myself thinking, "Now I have no excuse for not being a full-time, high-powered professional woman." I felt as if I had to leave home along with the kids. It seemed I could no longer enjoy the freedom of puttering around house and yard if the kids were not there to justify it. I remembered my sister-in-law making a similar comment when her children moved away. She was overwhelmed with anxiety and said, "I've always used the children as an excuse for not taking on a top professional position, and now I'll have to do that." My husband provided the appropriate question to both of us: "But why? To whom do you need to excuse yourself? Who says you have to get out there and make it professionally if you aren't kept at home by children's needs?"

I could see that the pressure came from within, from some should-sense that was very much influenced by feminist beliefs. A woman is supposed to go for it, to achieve. I was comparing myself to women in my field who attract big crowds and make big bucks, who seem chic and confident. As long as the boys were home, I could tell myself I didn't have time for that. But now I felt the full force of that image as a demand.

Women who have been full-time homemakers may struggle with a more severe version of the same dilemma. Lacking any image of what they can do or be apart from being a mother, they may feel their life has no meaning at all. The mental void, brought about by the absence of children, seems filled with a sense of worthlessness. I remember a mother of seven coming for counseling help because she thought she was going crazy. Shortly after her seventh child left home, she found herself on her knees in the garden planting azaleas. "I hate gardening," she said. "I have no interest in flowers at all. So what was I doing out there planting azaleas?" It made perfect sense to me. Gardening is another form of nurturing growing things. Why wouldn't a mother of seven, finding her home empty after all those years, feel a need for an alternative form of nurturing?

Our Graduation, As Well As Our Kids'

But all of this sense of loss and fear of the future comes from the narrow, human context of thinking. If we have used our motherhood as a school for Love, we find that the whole curriculum has prepared us for this graduation. Each expansion of our children's lives has expanded our consciousness of the limitless good of divine Life.

Anne Morrow Lindbergh goes on to say, "All the inner and outer exploration a woman has done earlier in life pays off when she reaches the abandoned shell."[17] The more we have placed the "center of gravity" in Life rather than in personal self, the less traumatic is the release of daily mothering. It is only the fragmented level of seeing that is subject to the incessant push and pull of comings and goings, each of which seems a crisis to the poor little person-sense. Allowing fragmentation to define our thinking and feeling will not only mean suffering for us but is likely to impact negatively on our children's unfoldment as well. The sense of freedom and joy that belong to the completion of high school can be substantially sabotaged by a clinging or morose mother. So this is the time to capitalize on the marvels we have accumulated over nearly two decades of motherhood.

Life has neither discontinued nor interrupted Its substance and Its activity, however much personal sense may be shouting "loss" and "ending" in our thinking. We have already discovered motherness/childness as qualities of Life, and it follows that they cannot be lost nor come to an end. My personal sense of being abandoned as mother and/or child, of losing contact with these aspects of myself as the children moved away, reveals itself to be impossible when viewed from the window of Spirit. What is required for relief from the sense of abandonment and worthlessness is radical spiritual logic, staying with the premise of one Life, the wholeness of Good, and not letting the human sense get away with its misconceptions.

During the first two or three months, I found myself often teary, but once I had recognized that the tears were those of the human misconception of motherhood, I could take issue with them. I could understandingly declare, "I am not crying," while tears ran down my cheeks. It's not that there's anything wrong with feeling human emotions, but there is no need to allow a universally hypnotic illusion to live its misery through us. We are not responsible for the misconceptions that claim to be our thinking and feeling and life story. We never chose those beliefs, nor would we, given other options. So I often ask myself, "Why should I passively go along with every miserable, sad thing that this false sense dreams up and calls me?"

The value of approaching motherhood as consciousness rather than as an interpersonal situation is proven a hundredfold as we are faced with the necessity to release our children into a larger sphere and move on ourselves. The fact that it feels very peculiar to us to no longer be mentally oriented to our children's comings and goings does not mean that it is a bad thing. It is just different.

The first half of the human story — moving out of our birth homes, completing school, finding jobs and mates and having and raising children — keeps us busy with what seem to be interpersonal issues. But the important people in our lives inevitably change or move away or die, and we learn that we must find our identity and foundation in something more lasting and substantial than other persons. Anne Morrow Lindbergh says, "Woman must come of age by herself — she must find her true center alone."[18]

The Age Factor

Age is a big factor for many women in the crisis of this period. Often menopause is occurring around the same time as the emptying out of the home. It is what these events symbolize in the context of the human life span that makes them so difficult for us. The end of daily mothering activities and the end of the biological capacity to bear children constitute a substantial death experience to the human sense of ourselves. It appears to be the end of creative, vital living. The seeming next big thing on the human life agenda is old age and death. I was speaking with a friend whose youngest girl goes off to college next year. We first exchanged details of our kids' activities and our own situations. She then blurted out, "I just had my fiftieth birthday, and I'm so depressed. Every day I cry and cry over getting old."

"What Am I Doing in My Grandmother's Body?"

Learning to see Life spiritually is the only help there is for the problem of human aging. We all come to feel like the eighty-year-old woman who said to her doctor, "I'm twenty-five. What am I doing in my grandmother's body?" *The very discrepancy between our consciousness of ourselves and the material evidence is proof to us that material sense is mistaken. It is evident that an aging, material body is not the ultimate truth of us, and that consciousness is where our true identity lies.* Our awareness has been vastly expanded through our years of motherhood. We have learned to see with the eyes of Love, to see the qualities of Goodness everywhere. Persons and bodies seem to exist on a time line. Years pass and wrinkles come, cosmetic wonders to the contrary notwithstanding. But qualities do not age. In fact, the dissolving of personal misconceptions that has taken place over our years of mothering results in much greater clarity of quality Life in our thinking. We are more loving, wise, beautiful, gracious, and vital now than when our first baby arrived, no matter what the time-lie declares. This recognition is of great value to us, and it enables us to stay centered in a way that is important to our young adult children.

Motherhood Is Far from Obsolete

One surprising discovery for me has been the degree to which young people depend upon the stability of the home base as they move from home to college or apartment. Kids may act and talk very confidently and be eager to make the move. But much of the confidence is based on the sense of home and parents remaining constant. A friend of our boys went away to college. A month later his parents came for a weekend and informed him that they were divorcing. They had stayed together until he was through high school, but since he was now gone, they were going ahead with their lives. This sounds like a perfectly reasonable way of doing things. The parents obviously cared about the boy's feelings in staying together while he lived at home. Nonetheless, the boy was devastated, did poorly at school, and finally dropped out in the first quarter of his second year.

Watching this boy's struggle to find his footing made me realize that motherhood is not at all obsolete, just because children are out of the home. My perception of the boys as "now gone" is not their perception of their situation. Home is still home, a steady base from which they begin to experiment with independence, but to which they want to feel they can return.

A Transition Period Requiring Our Flexibility

This transition period in the young people's lives requires a good deal of flexibility on our part. Struggling with our own ambivalence, it is not easy to remain responsive to both sides of their needs: to be welcoming when they come home and supportive when they leave. Yet I have found that the boys' somewhat random in-and-outness during the past year has helped break up the mesmerism of the mother-drama. Just when the sad scenario of loss would captivate me, the boys would be home for a weekend, their friends ensconced in the living room and their laundry on the floor by the washer. About thirty minutes after their arrival, I would be ready for them to leave again.

When Young Adults Are Unable To Leave Home

The flip side of the crisis of children leaving the home is the crisis of grown children failing to leave the home, or returning home to live after graduating from college. Cultural as well as individual factors combine to make it difficult for many young adults to get happily established on their own. Several of my friends have struggled over a period of years with how to help their children move out. The trouble is that the question, "How can I help my kid become independent?" is a contradiction in terms. In human terms, parental help and kids' independence tend to mutually exclude each other. Our very concern with helping our children may work against their developing the requisite sense of assurance that they can make it apart from us.

Like toddlers, young adults are subject to strong pulls in two directions: staying in the supportive home atmosphere and moving out into the freedom of being on their own. College bridges this gap by placing their independent

160   Mothering as a Spiritual Journey

existence in the context of a guiding and supporting structure. When kids have to face going directly from parental support to the complete independence of working and supporting themselves, it is a bigger shift and one that may seem very scary to them. The way we now support our kids is by encouraging and celebrating their unfolding maturity. Loving to see them going new places and doing new things blesses them and helps to carry us beyond the personal desire to cling.

When young people seem unable to leave home, there is always a factor of attachment on our part. We long to have them out of the house and to be free from the financial drain, yet we also dread the end of feeling needed and useful. A mother I know, who worries that her twenty-one-year-old son lives at home with no clear direction, nonetheless notices how much she delights in keeping the orange juice container full for him. She says, "It makes me happy that he can always count on his juice being there and it makes me feel useful that I am the one who provides it." Mothers are privileged to have an occupation that provides such immediate, if small, gratifications. We enjoy being needed, feeling important to our children's welfare. This makes us easily seduced into supporting the very dependencies that we want our young adult children to get beyond. "Why don't you grow up?" are words spoken by multitudes of exasperated parents, but such exasperation often masks our dread of losing the familiar and enjoyable aspects of daily parenthood.

A friend whose twenty-three-year-old son continued to live at home finally set a deadline for him to find an apartment and move out. She was loving and encouraging but firm throughout the process, and he finally found an apartment that he could afford. When moving day came, he moved, with his mother's help, despite vomiting up his breakfast. Three months later, she reported, he was happy and proud of being on his own, and talked about the move as if it had been his own idea!

Money often seems to be the issue that makes it impossible for young adults to move out from their parental home. A friend's daughter has returned home after graduating from a prestigious college because she hasn't yet found a job that pays enough to enable her to support herself. "Does she pay rent?" I asked. "Well, no," said her mother. "She was doing temporary work when she moved in and was earning so little that it didn't seem to make sense to have her pay rent. But now I think I should have charged her something right from the beginning, even if it was only $3 a week."

How do we know what to do in such situations? It is no different now than when we were wondering how to handle toilet training or music lessons or a curfew time. There is no one right way to do the transition period. But Life remains lawful and of the same substance as always. *Knowing that Love is never unintelligent nor Intelligence unloving, we will be less likely to invite young adults to take advantage of us.*

We do not need so much to get tough with our kids as to be clear with ourselves. Young adults need to be making their own discoveries, finding a base apart from their childhood home. And we need to be letting quality Life come in new forms and experiences. We consider proposed living arrangements in this light. Asking ourselves, "Who really profits from this arrangement?" helps us see what is needed for all concerned and keeps us from going with situations that simply mollify human attachment feelings.

Mothers and Young Adults
Face the Same Sort of Crisis

The young adult's crisis of leaving home is made of the same ingredients as the mother's crisis of being left. The anxiety is based on identity concerns. The mother does not know, with confidence, who she is apart from the mother identity/function that has centered her life for decades. The young person does not yet know, with confidence, who he or she is, apart from the family. We all feel anxious and insecure, facing unknown situations in the belief that we are separate persons in charge of our lives. No wonder we cling to each other!

Just as many aspects of becoming a mother seemed hard or unpleasant to us at the beginning, so there is an adjustment period to go through as our children reach adulthood, which does not feel comfortable to human sense. I feel greatly blessed to have a friend going through the throes of being a new mother right now, because It puts the whole motherhood scene in perspective. I sit and chuckle to myself as I see her moaning and groaning about getting used to the very presence and dailiness of motherhood tasks which, twenty years from now, she will inevitably find difficult to give up. It is so helpful to see the whole human dilemma as a sort of existential joke. We are always being called upon to get used to something new only, it seems, to be called upon to give it up and move on to something else. Noticing this, we can see how crucial it is not to take personal details too seriously. It is best to laugh at our mother-stuff and laugh at our kids' kid-stuff.

At no time is there a greater need to understand that Life is spelled with a capital "L," that is, that we do not have separate material and personal lives of our own to manage. As mothers, we have had two decades of learning the lovely lessons of the oneness and wholeness of reality. We are thus prepared to help our young people learn that they don't have to trust themselves. Human selfhood is not trustworthy. But Life is trustworthy, because It is lawful, and the law of Life is Love. The gifts in consciousness that our years of motherhood have furnished now become the basis of our ability to lovingly and intelligently release and encourage our kids.

Personal, bodily separation from our children does not mean that we become separate from those so-precious qualities of childness that have blessed and enriched our awareness. This is where spiritual understanding can deliver the most substantial of goods to us. *What we loved so dearly in and as our little children were qualities, not small bodies and immature minds. The qualities of playfulness, spontaneity, innocence, purity, and wonder are as true of Being today as when our children were little. They are as much in evidence now as then, because qualities are always in the eye of the beholder.* We do not need to lose the eye (I) of quality because the material picture changes.

Advanced Lessons

This stage of motherhood might be called Love's graduate school. Having watched Love unfolding itself as the harmonious growth and development of our children and ourselves, we are ready for advanced lessons. *Love never was and is not now something that persons exchange or provide. Love is the best word to describe the quality of consciousness that constitutes real Life. What we would humanly call "finding love" is always an unfoldment in consciousness and never a matter of the proximity or behavior of persons.* Our children did not provide us with either Love or childness, nor did they make us motherness. They merely illustrated, in an appreciable way, the truth of these qualities. So now we must again move beyond the comforts of our current self-image as mother to let our consciousness of Love expand. I have for years cherished and learned from a mother's description of her discovery of divine Love coincident to a breakthrough in her limited, personal sense of mother love. This event in consciousness took place when a noted spiritual leader simply looked lovingly at her children. She wrote:

> I wish I could make the world know what I saw when Mrs. Eddy looked at those children. It was a revelation to me. I saw for the first time the real Mother-Love, and I knew that I did not have it. I had a strange, agonized sense of being absolutely cut off from the children. It is impossible to put into words what the uncovering of my own lack of real Mother-Love meant to me.
>
> As I turned in the procession and walked toward the line of trees in the front of the yard, there was a bird sitting on the limb of a tree, and I saw the same love, poured out on that bird that I had seen flow from Mrs. Eddy to my children. I looked down at the grass and the flowers and there was the same Love resting on them. It is difficult for me to put into words what I saw. This Love was everywhere, like the light, but it was divine, not mere human affection.
>
> I looked at the people milling around on the lawn and I saw it poured out on them. . . . I saw, for the first time, the absolute unreality of everything but this infinite Love. It was not only everywhere present, like the light, but it was an intelligent presence that spoke to me, and I found myself weeping as I walked back and forth under the trees and saying out loud, "Why did I never know you before? Why have I not known you always?"[19]

This mother underwent, spontaneously, the transformation in consciousness that is the work of this graduation period of motherhood. The shift is made from loving one's children personally to seeing Love in its transcendental dimensions. In the presence of true Mother-Love, which is non-personal and universal, this mother found her human attachment sense of love exposed and dissolved: "I had an agonized sense of being absolutely cut off from the children."

Researching My Attachments

In working with this beautiful story, I often stop at this point and research my own consciousness on the issue of attachment. I have clearly seen a sense of attachment, rather than love, operate under the guise of love and produce its troublesome agenda for myself and for the boys. Particularly now, as they move out, I can watch a desire for personal recognition and appreciation as a mother produce resentment and insist on the right to take them to task for their failures in this regard. Usually, because I can spot the difference between attachment and love, I can refrain from acting on the false sense. It is a salutary exercise for a mother to notice personal attachment thoughts because unmasking them cuts through the self-righteousness and self-defensiveness that so cloud our awareness of what is really going on.

It was the capacity of the mother in the story to let human, personal mother sense be seen through that prepared her consciousness for the glorious vision of omnipresent, infinite Love. If she had felt the need to defend her mother love to herself, she would have missed out on the fireworks. She would have ended up with another one of those dreary little monologues such as, "What does *she* know about mothering, anyway. *I'm* the one with two children. *I'm* the one who knows how tough it is to be a mother.... "

The marvels of this phase of motherhood may seem hard-won but are worth holding out for. It is much like the beginning stage. Watching the friend who is a new mother struggle with panic, self-pity, and doubts about her capacities and whether the baby will enhance or destroy her life, I am struck again with the fact that motherhood's crises, from first to last, lie wholly in the personal viewpoint. It is thinking of life as a personal story that has to be managed according to personal desires that gives rise to so much anxiety and torment.

Divine Love will never let us sit comfortably with less than Its fullness of Being. Expansion of consciousness is required of us. We either volunteer for duty, through the positive opportunities of Life, or we are drafted, through the problems that prove the human sense of things to be mistaken.

Discovering that Life is a substance of qualities governed by the law of Love is the only thing that will save us because it is the truth, and truth will have its fulfillment. *We start out just trying to keep our heads above water, interested in spiritual reality for the goods it can deliver to our human situation. But we realize, with every glimpse of Spirit, that the human approximation of good is the least of it. The consciousness of divine Good is not a means to a human end, but the end itself.* Thus, in learning to let God raise our kids,we have been raised from human life to divine Life, from earth to heaven, from the dim seeing of personhood to the radiant vision of universal Mind. "For now we see through a glass, darkly; but then, face to face: now I know in part, but then shall I know even as also I am known" (1 Cor. 13:12).

Forgiveness: Release from the Prison of Regret

Nothing keeps us imprisoned in the past like a sense of regret. Pictures of past mistakes, failures, and hurts continue to push for resolution. If we or our kids feel that we have not given or gotten what we should have, to or from each other, the tendency is to hang on and keep working at it. Unfortunately, however, personal sense doesn't know any other way to go about things than the one that has proven unsatisfactory in the first place. So nothing gets resolved; old patterns just keep repeating.

But the past isn't past. It is a present picture in consciousness. And, we have learned, present pictures in consciousness are best resolved in consciousness, not in a seeming external, interpersonal world. When I remember some scene from the past with discomfort — for me they usually involve our first son, since the second boy had the benefit of what I learned with his older brother — it gives me great joy to be able to resee it from the standpoint of the truth of Being. It is never too late to offer the whole human motherhood/childhood scene up to light of divine Good. Perhaps this is the biggest marvel of all: the release of all guilt and regret in the practice of spiritual forgiveness. Forgiveness means giving up something for something else. We give up negative memories, grudges, guilts, for the sake of a realization of the ultimate Goodness of divine Life.

A mother whose adult daughter was involved in psychotherapy was shocked when the girl, who had become very hostile and estranged, blurted out, "I always wanted a black dress, and you never would let me have one!" No matter how hard we've tried to be good mothers, personhood always has its gripes, on both sides of the mother/child dyad. The black dress gripe is just one picture of a sense of having been deprived. We don't need to feel either guilty or defensive about such accusations. The picture calls for correction, healing, and this is done in consciousness on the basis of truth, not interpersonally on the basis of good intentions. The mother cannot make her daughter forgive her, but she can forgive her daughter. She can give up the picture of an accusing, angry, perhaps deprived daughter in the acknowledgment that God has always been the only Mother/Father and therefore Love has always been the true substance of her daughter's experience.

Human children and human parents always feel deprived and misunderstood by each other. But is this what Mind knows? Is this what Life lives? Is this what Love is seeing? *We take our earthly experience to heaven when we subject it to the scrutiny of the ultimate standpoint of seeing. No matter what the seeming failures and sorrows of the human past, the divine Life is all that has ever been true, all that will ever be true.* Seeing this, we no longer offer negative memories the energy and support of calling themselves our experience. They then fall away for lack of identity. As this happens, such mental pictures lose their clarity in the consciousness of others, as well as in our own. In this way, the past can literally be erased.

The transformation of the past by present seeing is illustrated in the experience of a woman who had been a Zen student for five years. At the end of a particularly intensive meditation period, personal sense was broken through. She writes:

The lines written by a Christian mystic appeared in my head:

> All shall be well
> and all shall be well
> and all manner of things
> shall be well . . .

Yes! I thought. And not only *shall* all be well, all is well *right now*! And always had been well, only I had been too blind to see it. The incredible combination of fortunate circumstances that had led me to this moment, including all those I had considered blackest misfortune: the injured back, the writer's block, the spells of depression, family difficulties, delays in being accepted as a member of the Center, lost letters, knees that swelled and refused to bend, the move to far-off Mexico — all formed an intricate and loving pattern leading me to Zen, to this moment, preventing a head-long impetuosity that this middle-aged frame could not have supported, teaching me patience, feeding me disappointments and humiliations at a pace I could absorb, carrying me forward exactly in the right way, for me. And I knew the same miracles were unfolding for everyone.[20]

The Fulfillment of the Journey:
The Marvel of Divine Completeness

By the time our children are leaving home, we have had the kind of long-term experience that enables us to make the same sort of observations as the Zen student. We have seen that the sharp pains, fears, and disappointments of a moment do not give us an accurate reading of the reality of things. There is a larger Scheme, with Its own agenda and pattern, being, and unfolding in and around us and our little family stories.

The fulfillment of the spiritual journey of motherhood lies in the increasing release of the entire package of belief that we have been human mothers with human children who knock us for a loop on the way into our lives and knock us for a loop again on the way out. Love, intelligence, receptivity, nurturing, tenderness, purity, innocence, spontaneity, and joy are infinite and eternal aspects of the one Life. They may and do appear in any form and language that is appreciable to us at our level of understanding, from having mothers to being mothers, from being children to having children. But *the Good is all, from first to last, Life's celebration of Its own Being, Mind's knowing of Its own delightful ideas, Love's cherishing of Its own loveliness.* We don't do it, get it, have it, or lose it. As we are aware of it, the sense of ourselves as separate entities fades out. That one Life is our living, that Mind our knowing, that Love our seeing, here and now.

Motherhood and Culture

Mother qualities are such central aspects of Life that they can never be hidden by human cultural distortions for long. The legitimate feminist concern with equality for women often unwittingly promoted masculine values. But the impulsion of the feminine to express is everywhere in evidence. This impulsion has a lovely symbol in the presence of Barbara Bush as first lady. Her significance as the embodiment of mother qualities was recognized in a *Time* magazine article about the Wellesley College protest over her appointment as commencement speaker in May 1990:

> Bush may be the perfect antidote to this culture, which economist Sylvia Hewlett, author of *A Lesser Life,* says has "taught young women to almost despise the nurturing role." Indeed, now that Bush is on her own, she is holding her own. Rather than hype fashion designers or choose new White House china ... Bush spends her days drawing attention to the homeless, AIDS patients, the poor, and those whose lives have been so impoverished they never learned to read.
>
> For Wellesley students, says Hewlett, Bush "has all sorts of wisdom about what half of their lives will be" — of the victories of motherhood, small and evanescent, which occur largely behind closed doors with results apparent in the next decade, not the next deal. It is a profession in which almost nothing happens day by day but everything is won or lost over time. Impor-

tant stuff for these women who, if they are lucky, will graduate to more than a paycheck.[21]

Cultures in which motherhood qualities become obscured by personal beliefs lose their stable foundation. The importance of good mothering is being brought to the surface as an issue of great social significance in our culture right now, particularly in the poverty culture. As teenage girls, themselves largely unmothered, keep their babies, the need for new expressions of motherness is great. The social cost of letting mother qualities take a back seat to everything from war to drugs to personal achievement is coming home to us.

Social Role for Experienced Mothers

Experienced mothers provide a vast resource on two levels. Most important is our work in consciousness. We can see that the human picture of inadequately mothered children becoming even more inadequate mothers is a pathetic misconception of what is actually, always and everywhere, the fullness of Life. Every time that picture presents itself to us, we can see right through it to the presence of God's Father, Mother, and Child qualities.

This work in consciousness cannot help but show up in the discovery of available resources to meet the needs. I can envision a Mothers' Corps, like the Peace Corps, consisting of experienced mothers who would be paired with the child-mothers to provide the young women with nurture and support and to illustrate mature mothering with the babies. I have read of similar programs already being conducted.

Though focusing in this book on the role of motherhood, I have noticed that mother qualities may be expressed through any profession and through either gender. And I notice that whenever manifested, mother qualities are a blessing. Mother mentality looks to affirm, support, encourage, nurture. This quality of consciousness is needed not only in education and not only in working with children. Everyone does better when approached from such a standpoint, so mother mentality is an enhancement wherever it is present. When we live as this seeing and being of Life's lovingness, we are in this world as a blessing. Nothing could be more fulfilling.

A "Mothers For" Perspective

It is not accidental that groups have formed such as Mothers Against Drunk Driving and Mothers Against War. Motherness, with its nurturing nature, cannot help being against such human horrors. But my vision is for the increasing rise of a "Mothers *for*" perspective. This may or may not take the form of a specific movement. But it is something we graduate mothers can commit ourselves to individually, as a way of life. It is a way of seeing things, wherever we are. Motherseeing is always *for* every positive aspect of Life. It is for the Good, everywhere, all the time. Not only can we raise children who are aware of their quality identities, but we can nurture that awareness in everyone we meet through our responses. We can stand for quality in every aspect of society. And we can be sure that nothing goes farther toward ending war, ending drunkenness, ending drug use and all the other plagues of human sense, than does the realization of quality Good as the truth of our lives.

A Marvelous Thing Happened
on My Way to the End of This Book

The idea to write this book arose out of my own experience of the crisis of loss as the boys went to college. It started out being a sort of working through of my problem. But, like the raising of children, it soon became a discovery and unfoldment process clearly not being run by me. The idea that motherhood is the discovery and expression of divine qualities was not something that I had consciously formulated when I started to write. It clarified itself to me in the process of writing and rewriting the book. I sat down to record the experience of mothering as a spiritual journey and the journey continued, as concepts for what I had experienced revealed themselves. In this way, Mind makes available to the readers of the book what before was simply my own subjective experience.

Moreover, the book ends up being my own experiential proof that motherhood is a mental rather than interpersonal reality, for writing it has kept me "mothering" and enjoying child qualities just as much as when the boys were at home. In fact, it has been an even more effortless and pure form of participating in those qualities. No dirty diapers. No report cards or squabbles or car pooling. Just hours upon hours of enjoying ideas and memories and insights as they come up in consciousness.

It seems appropriate, therefore, to repeat the statement of gratitude with which I began the book, but here introduced by a blessing. *May the truth of divine Motherness and Childness shine in every mother's heart so that, finally, only gratitude remains.*

> I am grateful to have had the opportunity to let motherhood qualities be expressed through me. I feel so much enriched and secured by the seeing and being that have taken place because of being a mother. Despite my personal fears and tightness and grouchiness, Love has looked lovingly through my eyes at my children; intelligence has responded helpfully to their needs; vi-

tality has joined them in their adventures and their play.

To the eye of one unfamiliar with children, they often appear as an unknown species. I have loved seeing the masks of unfamiliarity dissolve, so that babies and toddlers and little kids and big kids and teenagers and young adults now all seem like friends to me, not strangers. My own children have made me one with all children.

I am grateful to have had the opportunity to let childness qualities fill my adult years. I am more flexible, open, spontaneous, and playful because of having had children. And, though it may seem contradictory, I am also more mature, centered, decisive, and sure of myself. There is no conflict, spiritually, between childness and maturity; they are two aspects of the completeness of Being.

I am grateful to have had the expansion of consciousness invited and evoked and cajoled in the positive and delightful ways that only motherhood provides.

The crises of our human experience, once past, seem never to have happened, but the marvels discovered not only remain but potentiate further seeing. We graduate from being pushed along by crises to cherishing the divine standpoint in consciousness for its own sake.

How lovely is thy dwelling place, O Lord of hosts.... Blessed are those who dwell in thy house, ever singing thy praise! (Ps. 84:1, 4).

❧

MOTHER'S RESOURCE GUIDE for Chapter 6

A Poem

Among my mother's belongings, I found a slim volume of poems: *Love Songs*, by Sara Teasdale. In the front my mother had written her name and the date: 1918. She was twenty-four years old when she bought this book.

The poems are delicate and beautiful, and they have given me a blessed reminder of the quality of my mother's consciousness. Even in an old age clouded by physical incapacity and worry, she retained a remarkable ability to see beauty. I have come to consider that her greatest gift to me.

Certain poems are marked with a faintly visible check, indicating that they were her favorites. The first poem in the book is so marked, and it has become a favorite of mine. It makes a very good meditation.

BARTER

Life has loveliness to sell,
All beautiful and splendid things,
Blue waves whitened on a cliff,
Soaring fire that sways and sings,
And children's faces looking up
Holding wonder like a cup.

Life has loveliness to sell,
Music like a curve of gold,
Scent of pine trees in the rain,
Eyes that love you, arms that hold,
And for your spirit's still delight,
Holy thoughts that star the night.

Spend all you have for loveliness,
Buy it and never count the cost;

For one white singing hour of peace
Count many a year of strife well lost,
And for a breath of ecstasy
Give all you have been, or could be.[22]

Notes

Chapter 1: The Marvelous Journey of Motherhood

1. Hugh Prather, *A Book of Games* (Garden City, N.Y.: Doubleday & Co., 1981), 1.

Chapter 2: Infancy

2. Kahlil Gibran, *The Prophet* (New York: Alfred A. Knopf, 1968), 17.
3. Thomas Hora, *In Quest of Wholeness*, 110. Out of print.
4. Polly Berends, *Whole Child/Whole Parent* (New York: Harper's Magazine Press, 1975), 226–27.
5. Alan A. Aylwin, "Be Still and Know . . . ," *The Christian Science Sentinel*, June 6, 1977.

Chapter 3: Ages One–Four

6. Mary Baker Eddy, *Miscellaneous Writings* (Boston: Christian Science Publishing Society, 1925), 60–61.

Chapter 4: Ages Five–Twelve

7. Thomas Hora, *In Quest of Wholeness*, 118–20. Out of print.
8. Rudolph Dreikurs, *Children: The Challenge* (New York: Hawthorn Books, 1964).
9. Ann Linthorst, *Thus Saith the Lord: Giddyap* (Orange, Calif.: PAGL Press, 1986), 56, 62. Available from the author.
10. Thomas Hora, *Dialogues in Metapsychiatry*, reprinted (Orange, Calif: PAGL Press, 1986), 61–62; available from the author.
11. Hora, *In Quest of Wholeness*, 109.
12. Polly Berends, *Whole Child/Whole Parent*, rev. ed. (New York: Harper & Row, 1983), 116.
13. Margaret P. Montague, "Twenty Minutes of Reality," *The Atlantic*, May 1916.

Chapter 5: Teenage

14. Nora Holm, *The Runner's Bible* (Boston: Houghton Mifflin, 1943), 46–77.
15. Philip Kapleau, *The Three Pillars of Zen*, rev. and expanded ed. (Garden City, N.Y.: Anchor Press/Doubleday, 1980), 279–80.

Chapter 6: Young Adulthood

16. Anne Morrow Lindbergh, *A Gift from the Sea*, twentieth anniversary ed. (New York: Vintage Books, 1991), 133.

17. Ibid, 134.

18. Ibid.

19. Irving Tomlinson, *Twelve Years with Mary Baker Eddy* (Boston: Christian Science Publishing Society, 1973), 61.

20. Philip Kapleau, *Zen: Dawn in the West* (Garden City, N.Y.: Anchor Press/Doubleday, 1979), 142.

21. *Time*, May 7, 1990, 35.

22. Sara Teasdale, *Love Poems* (New York: Macmillan, 1917), 3.

Copyright Acknowledgments